D1280496

Will the Soviet Union Survive Until 1984?

Will the Soviet Union Survive Until 1984?

By ANDREI AMALRIK

INTRODUCTION BY LEOPOLD LABEDZ

PREFACE BY HENRY KAMM

COMMENTARY BY SIDNEY MONAS

PERENNIAL LIBRARY
Harper & Row, Publishers
New York and Evanston

This work was first published in the Russian language by the Alexander Herzen Foundation, Amstel 268, Amsterdam-C, The Netherlands.

Contents

Introduction

by Leopold Labedz

THE NAME OF ANDREI AMALRIK was not so long ago totally unknown in the West; after the publication of his essay, "Will The USSR Survive Until 1984?," he became world famous. What is it that makes his case unique in the history of Soviet post-Stalin intellectual dissent?

Certainly not just the essay's thesis itself, which was intended as a statement of probabilities and not as a prophecy. No doubt its formulation and controversial nature largely accounted for the widespread interest in Amalrik in the sensation-hungry West, even though many did not agree with his conclusions. Yet the significance of the Amalrik phenomenon transcends the question of whether he is correct in his prognostications on the future Sino-Soviet war and the not-so-distant collapse of the Soviet empire. Amalrik's other writings (included in this volume) and his subsequent fate make it abundantly clear that we are confronted here with an unusual combination of high intelligence and civic courage, a combination which morally and intellectually ranks with the cases of Pasternak, Solzhenitsyn, and Sinyavski. While these authors have different outlooks and achievements, their "crime" of indulging in independent thought under a system which prescribes correct ideas and conclusions makes them into "cases" and provides the common thread between them.

When Pasternak's case occurred, the late Isaac Deutscher referred to him as "the voice from the grave." He asserted that Pasternak was a fossil from the prerevolutionary past, an internal Bourbon cut off from current Soviet reality, a man who did not and could not have any links with the Soviet present or future. The Amalrik case, coming as it does after a long series of dissenting voices among young Soviet intellectuals, is a particularly vivid proof of the fallacy of this kind of view. The whole history of Soviet intellectual dissent testifies to this: today we see the growing volume of the underground *samizdat* publications in which Pasternak's spiritual descendants are trying to emancipate themselves from the doctrinal perversities imposed on the Soviet mind.

In this process they inevitably manifest continuity with the Russian past. Already the specters of Slavophiles and Westernizers are stalking the scene. However, such traditional intellectual attitudes are very unevenly mixed among and inside individuals. For obvious reasons (the main one being Soviet cultural isolation during the last fifty years) there is a heavy preponderance of the Slavophile tradition. This is clearly visible both in Solzhenitsyn and Sinyavski.

It is fascinating to see a manifestation of the opposite tendency in Amalrik. He is, of course, not the pure embodiment of the Westernizing tradition, for he is too Russian for that. Also, he is very individualistic in his attitudes and thought, and one cannot reduce him simply to a "type," even a Weberian "ideal type." But subject to this *caveat* it is clear that for the first time we are witnessing a Western style of thinking in one of the prominent Soviet dissenters.

The appearance of the historical Russian attitudes among young Soviet intellectuals is, of course, not just a repetition of history; it is much more than that. The Soviet intellectual trying to throw off his mental shackles has to go through a complex psychological process to rid himself of a myriad of specifically Soviet conditioned reflexes. To overcome these he has to break a number of taboos. Amalrik demonstrates how far this process can go inside the Soviet system. The very existence of his type of writings, coming as it does from the Soviet Union, shows how radical the break can be and how successful can be the intellectual emancipation of a critical mind, in spite of all the political and social conditioning.

Admittedly Amalrik is a very special individual; he is probably the most un-Soviet mind at present in the Soviet Union. But his appearance can only be a source of puzzlement to those who either start from Deutscherian premises in their perception of Soviet developments, or who think in paranoid stereotypes characteristic of the reactionary Western or Russian emigré types.

In his personal comment on Amalrik's "Will The USSR Survive Until 1984?," the former *Washington Post* correspondent in Moscow, Anatole Shub, wrote (*Survey,*

Winter-Spring 1970):

Before living in Russia, I would have strongly doubted whether such a mind could exist and develop under Soviet conditions—in the same way that, for so many years, so many outsiders were certain that "Abram Tertz" could not possibly be a young Russian literary critic, but had to be an old Jewish communist or (as some said) a Pole. Even now, when Amalrik has become a world figure, many of the kindest, best-intentioned Western scholars find it incredible that he could have developed—*independently*—not merely an original mind, but a remarkable grasp of the Western thinking about his country.

However, some less kindly critics started a veritable smear campaign in the West, saying that Amalrik is a *Komitet Gossudarstvemnoi Bezopastnosti* agent. Articles to that effect were published in the American, German and the Russian emigré press. They were reproduced or reported all over the world.

It was a shameful episode. Here was a young and re-markable Soviet intellectual who had attained the high-est degree of individual emancipation from the Soviet mental universe, and whose personal philosophy was matched by his conduct in life, being crucified in the Western press for his originality and heroism. Anatole Shub remarked in his essay on Amalrik that this was not "the first example of Westerners doing the KGB's job for it," and he added:

Even if I did not myself have ample grounds for confidence in his integrity, even had I never met Andrei Amalrik, the word of that authentic hero, Pyotr Yakir, would be more than enough for me—certainly as against the insinuations of sneaky character assassins who hide behind the privileged anonymity of Western "analysts" and their dossiers, usually containing the Emperor's new clothes. The only words for such people are Russian: "*Kak vam ne stydno?*" (Have you no shame?).

It was fortunate that, before his arrest, Andrei Amalrik managed to rebut the aspersions on his character published in the West. His two replies to his Western "critics" are included in this volume. They make poignant reading now that he is in prison. He must have felt very bitter when he tried, in a restrained and dignified manner, to make clear to all those who are not intellectually primitive and morally deaf that, as he put it, "it would be too great an honor for the KGB to have such people as myself among its collaborators."

His detractors were particularly insistent on one point (the first to make it was a certain Mr. Henry S. Bradsher from the Washington *Evening Star*). In spite of the publication of his "anti-Soviet" writings in the West, Amalrik was not arrested, and this, they implied, constitutes a proof that he is either a KGB man or is being used by it. Since Amalrik's arrest we have not heard from these critics, although on their premises it should constitute a proof of his innocence. They can of course now come forward with the argument that the arrest itself was a put-on KGB job, but they have not yet done so. It is easy to understand Amalrik's feelings and his bitter irony about the "argument" used by his detractors:

My arrest is a kind of litmus paper which is to indicate whether I am a KGB agent or not. As far as I could understand, Mr. Bradsher is not the only man who thinks like this.

To pose the question in such terms seems to me extremely immoral. My country is not a Roman arena. I am not a gladiator, and the Western world, in the name of which Mr. Bradsher begins to speak with pathos towards the end of his article, is not Roman plebs, watching excitedly or coolly to see whether the gladiator will really die or whether it is only a circus trick.

When I was writing my books and intending to hand them over for publication, I realized that I was risking imprisonment; I was ready for it and I am ready for it now. But I thank God for every day of freedom which is given to me and which I spend at home with my wife. It seems to me that an honorable man who believes in God should not say: "He has not yet been arrested—that is very suspicious," but rather: "Thank God he has not yet been arrested, that means there is one more free man on earth."

Amalrik predicted that the KGB would arrest him in its own good time, and so it did on May 21, 1970 when he was staying in his dilapidated country cottage near the village of Akulovo, 85 miles southeast of Moscow. Both the cottage and his room in Moscow were thoroughly searched by the KGB men and five of Amalrik's manuscripts, as well as other "subversive" items (such as a copy of the Dutch edition of his book), were confiscated. Despite a number of Western protests by fellow historians and intellectuals, no indications were forthcoming from the Soviet Union about Amalrik's prospects under Brezhnev's "socialist legality."

However, we have heard in the West his real voice, and it was not "a voice from the grave." He had been interviewed shortly before his arrest by a correspondent in Moscow, William Cole, who shortly thereafter was expelled from the Soviet Union. The interview was filmed and taped in Moscow and later broadcast over the CBS Television Network (on July 26, 1970 in New York and by the BBC on August 28, 1970 in London), together with similar interviews with Pyotr Yakir and Vladimir Bukovsky.

In reply to Mr. Cole's questions, Amalrik expounded his views on the current situation in the USSR, clarified some of the points in his celebrated essay, and expressed, as things turned out, a justified doubt about his chances to remain free. He knew better than anyone the risks involved in his "un-Soviet" behavior. In the "Open letter to Kuznetsov" he wrote: "By living in this country and by continuing to write and do what I consider right, I can at any moment be sent to prison again or be dealt with in any other fashion." But as in his view "no oppression can be effective without those who are prepared to submit to it," he was ready to challenge individually the whole might of the Soviet state and provide an example of how a "free man can and should act" under conditions of oppression. In his opinion the Soviet totalitarian structure could disappear only if Soviet citizens lost their belief in its omnipotence and their fear of it. To break its magic spell, an individual must develop an "inner freedom" and deprive the oppressors of their weapon of fear which would not be effective against those who possess such "inner freedom."

This may appear somewhat quixotic as a guideline for the population at large, or even for intellectuals, few of whom are heroes or saints, but Amalrik stressed the personal character of his conclusions:

From childhood the regime under which I was compelled to live was organically alien to me: its culture seemed to be pitiful, its ideology false and the way of life foisted upon my fellow-citizens humiliating. I am an individualist by nature and my protest has always been a personal one. I always wanted to uphold my human worth and the right to be free myself. But I do not want to be understood as always thinking only of myself. I would like—and perhaps my example helps here—each of my fellow-countrymen also to feel the significance of his own personality. Only then, I think, is a struggle for common interests possible. Because a struggle for "common interests" by people with a slave psychology can and does lead only to common slavery.

Can personal example be all that powerful? Heroes and saints always thought so, but they have never in fact acted on pragmatic considerations alone. If Amalrik is indeed one of those "naturally superior human beings" of whom Solzhenitsyn writes, his present fate is not only to be a prophet without honor in his own country—this after all is proverbial—but also, as it may seem to him, abroad. It is said to reflect that Andrei Amalrik, persecuted and arrested in his Soviet fatherland, was also slandered in the West. Pasternak, Solzhenitsyn and Sinyavsky were at least spared this particular bitter cup.

In the present context of intensified cultural repressiveness in the Soviet Union and of the trendy "revolutionary" and isolationist moods among the American intelligentsia, the heartcry of Amalrik, even more pathetic now that he is behind prison bars, may not be "correctly understood," or even properly heard:

I hope that I will be understood in America, a country created by freedom-loving individualists who have come from all corners of the world. I hope that my books, read not between the lines, but exactly as I wrote them, will be the best answer to idle talk about them and to outright slander against me.

One can only hope that this will be the case. But one

cannot help detecting a note of political naiveté in this otherwise sceptical mind. One cannot help noticing the ironical juxtaposition of Amalrik's fate and that of the American "revolutionaries" like Jerry Rubin and Abbie Hoffman. He, an authentic rebel facing a real political oppression, is awaiting in prison what can only be a mock trial; they, the TV "revolutionary heroes" who mocked American judicial procedure, are, as a result, so much in demand that they are receiving sizable earnings on their (illiterate) writings and lecturings. Clearly, "doing it" has different consequences for the individuals concerned in the USSR and the USA.

How will future historians see in retrospect the Orwellian date of 1984? Will they look back on the next decade as a period of competitive decadence for the two giants? Or will there be a reversal of the present trends which would make an evolution towards a less Orwellian 1984 more likely? Amalrik's question can be asked about both countries, even though a negative reply may not be realistic about either of them. And the question is not only relevant to their internal developments, but also to the changes in their international status.

But whatever the case may be in 1984, it is altogether likely that by that time today's US "revolutionary heroes" will be forgotten, but Amalrik will not.

Portrait of a Dissenter

by Henry Kamm

IF ANDREI AMALRIK LIVED in the West—it is not his wish —he would probably be teaching history or literature at a university and contributing to scholarly journals while preparing some more solid piece of scholarship and writing satirical plays and essays on art and politics.

He would belong to no political party, but his voice would be heard in protest over moral issues transcending politics, such as the wars against Vietnam and Czechoslovakia, the suppression of democracy in Greece and the persecution of democrats in the Soviet Union.

He and his beautiful wife, Gyusel, would live in a spacious apartment in a part of town where artists live. Gyusel would have a room with big windows, where she could work on her stippled portraits and pursue her search for her own way to paint. There would be a quiet corner for Andrei's typewriter.

Books would be everywhere, and they would have been read, while visiting friends would feel free to take them home to read without asking. Their friends' paintings and drawings would hang or lean against the walls. The record player would be going most of the time, the music very old or modern.

Friends would be there day and night, feeling completely at home. They would be serious men and women who didn't take themselves too seriously, people like Andrei and Gyusel. The talk, even on the most weighty matters, would often be gay, and never heavy or melancholy. The subjects would be bigger than current politics. The teakettle would not run dry or grow cold.

The friends would bring their children, and Andrei and Gyusel would have their own, because they love children and have the gift of making them feel important.

But Andrei is a Russian, thirty-one years old, crew-cut and nearsighted, living in Moscow or sometimes in a cabin he and Gyusel have bought for a few rubles on a state farm. As he would if he lived in a freer country, Andrei lives by the urgings and dictates of his free conscience as much as he can.

His position is primarily moral. He sympathizes with the aims of the intellectual dissidents but does not sign their protests and petitions; his whole life is a dissent, private and unaffiliated, from a system that holds him but has no place for him.

"I was against the system when I was a child," Andrei has said. "My protest is not here—" pointing to his head —"but here." He jabbed a finger at his stomach. "It is organic. I am so opposed to the system that in reaction I want to do something with my hands.

"I am against the system not because it is dishonest but from organic revulsion. For example, I cannot listen to the Soviet radio. I cannot read *Pravda*. It is crude, stupid and full of lies."

His organic revulsion against untruth, his visceral inability to bow to the official dictate that he must accept deceit, would make life difficult for Andrei Amalrik anywhere in the world. In the Soviet Union it leaves him no choice but to be an outcast.

He has found his place and maintains his bearings by uncompromising adherence to his incorruptible vision of the truth. No pressure, no temptation, has deflected him from this path, which is as organic a part of him as his rejection of the system.

This has made him impervious to the blandishments of the KGB, the secret police, to make things easier for himself by informing occasionally on his friends, Russians or foreigners. This is why he cannot choose the road of Anatoly Kuznetsov, the novelist who defected to Britain.

Unlike Kuznetsov, Amalrik is incapable of accepting censorship of his writings, of countenancing the repression of some in order to let the rest be published. What Andrei writes is not tailored for possible publication in his country; he cannot trim his thought. And, again unlike Kuznetsov, he could not go through the pretense of collaborating with the KGB in order to be allowed to make the trip that would lead to freedom. Because for Andrei there is a higher freedom than that which Kuznetsov had to go to England to find. He explained this in an open letter to the recent defector:

What, in effect, threatened the Russian writer, if, before his first visit abroad, he had refused to collaborate with the KGB?

The writer would not have gone abroad, but he would have remained an honest man. In refusing to collaborate he would have lost a part, perhaps a considerable part, of his external freedom, but he would have achieved greater inner freedom.

I warmly and sincerely congratulate you on being now in a free country, and I hope this will be an important step for you on your path to inner freedom.

Andrei has this higher freedom, which he calls "inner," although he remains in the Soviet Union and plans to remain there. He has it because he has not even pretended to deliver so much as an atom of his mind and soul to the system. He sympathizes with tormented Soviet intellectuals, like Kuznetsov, who cannot give it their faith but feel that in order to live they must compromise. Andrei cannot do as they do.

"It seems to me that no oppression can be effective without those who are willing to submit to it," he wrote to Kuznetsov. "It sometimes appears to me that the Soviet 'creative intelligentsia'—that is, people accustomed to thinking one thing, saying another and doing a third—is, as a whole, an even more unpleasant phenomenon than the regime that formed it."

Andrei's freedom amid unfreedom baffles those of small mind, both in Moscow and in the West. Because he lives resolutely within Soviet law, the authorities have not found a way of silencing him. And because they have not silenced him, a few Western observers have suggested that Andrei is an agent of the secret police. It is difficult to see how they can believe this in the face of his public statements and writings—for instance, this book—which radically reject all that the Soviet Union professes to believe.

These observers do not understand that Andrei, having refrained from political activity or surreptitious distribution of his writings, has violated not a letter of even the most unjust Soviet law designed to silence opposition. Nor do they understand that human rights in his country have progressed to the point where political repression, while still almost universal, must be based upon law or covered by stretching existing administrative regulations.

He alluded to this in an open letter to Western newspapers protesting steps by the authorities to deprive him of most of his earnings from foreign publication of his works. With the wry boldness that marks all his dealings with the authorities, Andrei wrote:

"Stalin would have executed me for the fact that my books have been published abroad. His wretched successors dare only embezzle a part of my money. It only reaffirms my opinion of the degradation and decrepitude of this regime."

This is the public voice of a man whose life is wholly in the hands of the authorities speaking directly to those authorities. It is unlikely that they have heard such a voice before. Andrei is of a new generation, said Viktor Krasin, a more orthodox but in his own way equally bold dissident, sentenced at the end of 1969 to five years of exile. Krasin went on to say: "He fights the authorities. He confronts them directly. He does not have the fear of Stalin's labor camps in his bones."

Andrei's directness must make a similar impression on many of the older generation. But I do not believe that his frontal attack on the established order is prompted by an absence of fear. It stems rather, I think, from his individuality, from the fact that, unlike other dissidents,

Andrei is not fighting for a political cause. He is a man struggling for his integrity, his soul, his own truth, in a system that insists that each man must surrender his self and his soul and accept its truth.

As Luther, who also had no party, told the authorities who challenged his dissent, "Here I stand; I can do no other."

Although the authorities have not yet found a way of stilling Andrei, his freedom has not been without setback or hindrance. The price he has paid for being a free man in his native land—the only land he has ever known—is high.

By training and inclination he is a historian, the son of a man of similar interest and character, like himself thwarted by a system incapable of coping with individuals. Andrei is a historian without a university degree or teaching post and a writer whose works have not been published in his own country.

Even though none of the five plays he has written has been printed or performed in the Soviet Union, Andrei was imprisoned in 1965 on the charge that they were "anti-Soviet and pornographic." The case was eventually dropped, and he was let off instead with a sentence of two and a half years' exile in Siberia as a "parasite." That is the Soviet term for a man not employed in a regular job. Andrei prefers to be an occasionally employed historian and writer to giving up his real work and disappearing into a factory. Showing further magnanimity, the authorities ended his exile early.

Gyusel, a Tatar, followed Andrei into exile, voluntarily and at the cost of breaking with her family. They were married in Siberia. Because they did not have the ruble and a half for the marriage license, they hired themselves out for a day to a collective farm. The two rubles they earned paid for the license and sugar for their tea. In Siberia, Andrei worked as a shepherd and cart driver and Gyusel painted.

Though taking no part in organized protest, Andrei has consistently stood up for the causes in which he believes. At each of the trials of Soviet citizens persecuted for their convictions, Andrei is to be found among the small band of friends who request admission to the courtroom—officially, the trials are public—and when this is refused—as it always is—he does vigil outside, to show what side he is on.

In 1968 he surprised Soviet authorities when he and Gyusel spontaneously picketed the British Embassy because Britain was supplying arms to Nigeria for its war on Biafra. Spontaneous demonstrations, even against what the Soviet Union terms "imperialism," are unheard of in Moscow.

Andrei was expelled from Moscow University in 1963 for submitting a paper suggesting that an early Russian state centered at Kiev in the ninth century owed much of its civilization to the Normans and for taking this paper to the Danish Embassy to be forwarded to a Danish scholar of similar views. In the official opinion of his country, all Russia is a creation of Russians only.

Andrei refused to withdraw his conclusions, although the rest of his paper would have been accepted, and his formal education was promptly terminated.

Instead of their own apartment, Andrei and Gyusel occupy the sunless back room of a six-room flat in which six families share one kitchen, one toilet, one bathtub.

Andrei would doubtless write more and Gyusel get more painting done if all their living were not forced into the confines of these four walls.

There are fewer books than Andrei would like, because the choice of literature in his country is as narrow as his four walls. The last time I visited him, I arrived to find five surly men who had come with a warrant to search the bookshelves and drawers. This further reduced Andrei's library.

The chief searcher closely inspected my twelve-year-old daughter's shopping bag but found only a box of chocolates. After removing the wrapping and peering inside, he allowed Alison to give it to Gyusel, who is her friend and to whom she had come to say good-bye.

With most of their belongings scattered on the floor, where five secret policemen were pawing through them, Gyusel found a toy animal to give to my daughter in return. Then Andrei, ignoring the uninvited visitors, proposed tea to his American friends, and Gyusel, under guard, went to the communal kitchen to prepare it. Despite the police and the disorder, she insisted on the nicety of putting the sugar in a bowl before serving her friends.

Although Andrei and Gyusel must deny themselves much to maintain their self-respect, they have not denied themselves friends. Nor do they, in turn, deny themselves to their friends, as most Russians who have unorthodox friends occasionally do. They have the courage to invite into their room those whom, if they were more prudent or their consciences guilty, they would shun. But Andrei believes in living strictly by the laws of his country and not, like less courageous Soviet citizens, in drawing the limits of personal freedom to a safer compass than the law allows—and there is no law against receiving foreigners and their children.

So Andrei pays the price for remaining himself, and, out of love, Gyusel pays it with him. He has never had a job equal to his intelligence and talent, and she cannot become a member of the Union of Artists, which alone makes it possible officially to exhibit and sell paintings. Andrei has worked as a letter carrier, a proofreader, a construction worker (despite a frail body and a congenital heart ailment), a lighting technician in a film studio, a translator of technical literature, a laboratory helper, a cartographer, a private tutor and secretary and a timekeeper at sports events.

For a brief spell he was allowed to write articles on innocuous subjects for the press, but the secret police ended that. Presumably this enforced lack of regular employment makes it easier to designate him a shiftless "social parasite" and keep alive the threat of exile.

Andrei and Gyusel have no children. People who have to live outside their society must deny themselves not only material success but also infinitely greater joys. But they retain in return an awareness of truth, a sense of beauty and a free conscience.

And so Andrei can say of himself, as he looks out from his cabin, where he wrote this book, upon the country that he loves and that rejects him: "Now, patiently awaiting his return to prison, he occupies his time growing cucumbers and tomatoes."

Will the Soviet Union Survive Until 1984?

Will the Soviet Union Survive Until 1984?

I began to express my views about the approaching crisis in the Soviet system in the autumn of 1966, soon after my return to Moscow from exile in Siberia.[1]* At first I discussed these views only with some of my small circle of friends. Then, in November, 1967, I set down my thoughts in a letter which I sent to Literaturnaia Gazeta *(Literary Gazette) and to* Izvestia, *asking them to publish it. Both newspapers politely replied that they would not do so because they could not agree with some of the views I had expressed.*

Nevertheless, subsequent events both in this country and abroad convinced me that many of my assumptions were well founded, and I decided to put them down in an article. At first I thought of entitling it "Will the Soviet

* Editor's numbered notes may be found at the end of the text, beginning on page 91.

Union Survive Until 1980?" in the belief that 1980 was the nearest likely date in round numbers. In March, 1969, a reference to this appeared in the press: the Moscow correspondent of the Washington Post, Anatole Shub, briefly and not quite accurately described some of my views and cited the title of my article in progress. He referred to me as "a Russian friend." *

However, an expert on ancient Chinese thought and an admirer of modern English literature, to whom I, in turn, must refer only as "a Russian friend," advised me to change 1980 to 1984. I agreed willingly to the change, especially since it did not violate my preference for round figures: since it is now 1969, we are looking forward to a time exactly fifteen years hence.

My work on the article was somewhat hampered and delayed by a search of my apartment on May 7, 1969, during which certain books and documents necessary to the work were taken from me. Still, I consider it my pleasant duty to thank the agents of the KGB and the public prosecutor's office, who carried out the search, for not taking the manuscript of this article and thus making it possible for me to bring the work to a successful end.

Since I regard the conclusions reached here as in many respects debatable, I shall be grateful for constructive criticism. Interested readers who find it convenient may write to me directly at Vakhtangov Street 5, Apartment 5, Moscow G-2, U.S.S.R.

* *International Herald Tribune*, March 31, 1969 [Washington *Post*, June 15, 1969].

I HAVE UNDERTAKEN THIS STUDY for three compelling reasons.

The first is simply my interest in Russian history. Almost ten years ago, I wrote a work on Kievan Rus.[2] Due to circumstances beyond my control, however, I was forced to interrupt my researches on the origin of the Imperial Russian State; now, as a historian, I hope to be compensated for that loss by being a witness to the end of that state.

Second, I have been able to observe closely the efforts to create an independent social movement in the Soviet Union—a development that in itself is very interesting and deserves at least a preliminary assessment.

And third, I have been hearing and reading a great deal about the so-called "liberalization" of Soviet society. This idea may be formulated as follows: The situation is better now than it was ten years ago; therefore ten years from now it will be better still. I will attempt to show here why I disagree with this notion.

I must emphasize that my essay is based not on scholarly research but only on observation and reflection. From an academic point of view, it may appear to be only empty chatter. But for Western students of the Soviet Union, at any rate, this discussion should have the same interest that a fish would have for an ichthyologist if it suddenly began to talk.

I

It would appear that in the course of approximately five years, from 1952 to 1957, a kind of "revolution at the top" took place in our country. This revolution passed through such moments of intense strain as the creation of the so-called enlarged Presidium of the Central Committee of the Communist Party of the Soviet Union,[3] the "Doctors' Plot,"[4] the mysterious death of Stalin, the abolition of the enlarged Presidium, the purge of the state security organs, the mass rehabilitation of political prisoners and the public condemnation of Stalin, and the Polish and Hungarian crises of 1956. It ended with the complete victory of Khrushchev.

Throughout this period the country passively awaited its fate. While struggle was going on continuously "at the top," not a single voice "from below" was heard challenging the orders which at any given moment were handed down "from above." In actual fact, underground groups with opposition programs had already begun to appear—for example, the Krasnopevtsev group, which was arrested in 1956.[5] But because they were illegal and received no publicity, each group's protest actions were known only to its handful of members.

But the "revolution at the top" apparently loosened up the monolithic system created by Stalin and thus made possible some movement in Soviet society. Before the period was over, a new force, independent of the government, began to take shape. It may roughly be called the "Cultural Opposition."

Certain writers who until then had swum only in official waters or simply remained silent began speaking with new voices, and some of their works began to be published or were circulated in manuscript. There appeared on the scene many young poets, musicians, artists and writers of satirical lyrics who sang their own songs. Typewritten magazines began to circulate, semilegal art expositions were held and troupes of young actors, singers and entertainers were organized.*

This movement was directed not against the political regime as such but only against its culture, which the regime regarded as a component part of itself. Therefore the regime began to combat the Cultural Opposition, winning complete victory in case after case. Writers "repented," publishers of underground magazines were ar-

---

* Examples that come to mind are the publication of *Doctor Zhivago* by Boris Pasternak, the publication of the typewritten magazine *Syntax*[6] by Alexander Ginzburg, the public reading of poems in Moscow's Maiakovsky Square, exhibitions of independent artists like Anatoly Zverev and Oskar Rabin, the official publication of several novels, stories and poems that were later severely criticized, and the appearance of many singers and song writers like Okudzhava, Galich, Vysotsky and others whose songs circulated in millions of tape recordings. All were manifestations of widely differing levels of culture, but all were directed against "official" culture.

rested, art exhibitions were closed and poets were dispersed.

Nevertheless, victory over the Cultural Opposition as a whole was not achieved. On the contrary, the opposition was to some extent gradually absorbed into official art, its own nature being modified in the process; but by modifying official art in turn, it was able to preserve some of its identity as a cultural phenomenon. At the same time, by reconciling itself to the existence of a Cultural Opposition and virtually ignoring it, the regime robbed it of the political impact it had acquired as a result of the official struggle against it.

At this time, however, a new force emerged from within the Cultural Opposition; a force that stood not only against official culture but against many aspects of the ideology and practice of the regime. It emerged as a result of the crossing of two opposing trends: the striving of society to obtain greater social and political information and the efforts of the regime to control even more completely every aspect of information given to the public.

This new force came to be known as *"samizdat."** Novels, stories, plays, memoirs, articles, open letters, leaflets, shorthand records of official meetings and court

---

* *Samizdat* refers to work that is published by the author himself, and it is, in fact, a traditional Russian method of circumventing official censorship. Examples of present-day *samizdat* are the novels of Alexander Solzhenitsyn, the memoirs about life in prison camps of Yevgenia Ginzburg,[7] Mrs. Adamova and Anatoly Marchenko,[8] the articles of Anatoly Krasnov-Levitin,[9] the short stories of Varlaam Shalamov, the poems of Nataliia Gorbanevskaia,[10] and others. But it should be noted that a significant proportion of *samizdat* is anonymous. *Samizdat* also includes works that have been published abroad and were only later brought into the Soviet Union, such as the books of Andrei Siniavsky[11] and Yuli Daniel,[12] as well as books of foreign authors which have been either typed out or put on microfilm. Examples are the writings of George Orwell and Milovan Djilas and articles from foreign newspapers and magazines.

hearings in dozens, hundreds and thousands of typewritten copies and photostats began to circulate throughout the country.

Gradually, over a period of perhaps five years, the emphasis of *samizdat* shifted from literary to documentary works and acquired a steadily more pronounced social and political content. Naturally, the regime recognized *samizdat* as potentially more dangerous than the Cultural Opposition, and therefore it fights it with even greater vigor.

Examples of this struggle include the sentencing of Siniavsky and Daniel to seven and five years, respectively, of imprisonment in "strict-regime" labor camps for having published their books abroad (1965),[13] the sentencing of Viacheslav Chornovil to three years for compiling an account of political trials in the Ukraine (1967),[14] the sentencing of Yuri Galanskov to seven years for compiling the anthology *Phoenix*,[15] the sentencing of Alexander Ginzburg to five years for compiling a collection of documents on the trial of Siniavsky and Daniel (1968),[16] and the sentencing of Anatoly Marchenko to one year after he wrote his book on the prison camps of the post-Stalin era (1968).*

Nevertheless, *samizdat*, like the Cultural Opposition, gradually gave birth to a new, independent force which can already be regarded as a real political opposition to

---

* Severe measures are also taken against those who circulate the works of *samizdat*. For instance, the typist Vera Lashkova was sentenced to one year together with Ginzburg and Galanskov merely for having typed their manuscripts. Yuri Gendler, Lev Kvachevsky and Anatoly Studenkov were sentenced, respectively, to four years, three years and one year (in Leningrad) for reading and circulating literature that had not been passed by the censors (1968), and Ilia Burmistrovich was sentenced to three years (in Moscow) for the same offense (1969).

the regime or, at least, as a political opposition in embryo. This has turned into a social movement that calls itself the Democratic Movement. It can be regarded as a new phase in the opposition to the regime, and as a *political* opposition, for the following reasons:

First, although it has not adopted a definite organizational form, it regards itself as a movement and calls itself such, it has leaders and activists, and it relies on a considerable number of sympathizers. Second, it consciously sets itself specific aims and chooses particular tactics, although these are still diffuse. Third, it desires legal status and publicity for its activities, and works hard for such publicity. In this it differs from the small or even the large underground groups.*

Before examining to what extent the Democratic Movement is a mass movement and how well defined and attainable its aims are—that is, whether it is really a movement and whether it has any chances of success—it is worth examining the ideological foundations on which any opposition in the Soviet Union can be based.

Of course, as the author himself clearly remembers, even in 1952–56 there were a great number of people who

* Details about several groups of this sort have, despite the secrecy which surrounded their trials, become known since 1956: the group of Krasnopevtsev and Rendel, which was tried in 1956; the group of Osipov and Kuznetsov (1961); the group that published the magazine *Kolokol* (*The Bell*) in Leningrad (1964); the group of Dergunov (1967); and others. The largest of the underground organizations so far exposed has been the All-Russian Social-Christian Union for the Liberation of the People. Twenty-one members of this group were sentenced in Leningrad in 1967–68, although the Union's total membership was far greater.

were dissatisfied with the regime and opposed to it. But not only was this discontent of a drawing-room character; it also leaned heavily on a negative ideology: the regime was bad because it did or did not do this or that. The question of what was desirable was generally not asked. It was also assumed either that the regime was not living up to the ideology it professed or that the ideology itself was worthless. The search for a positive ideology forceful enough to oppose the official ideology did not begin until the end of this period.

This is a very interesting question, and my view of it may be mistaken since I do not know the full facts. For very obvious reasons it is simply impossible to know them. They will become known only with the publication of the postwar archives of the KGB. I do not intend to suggest that there were no individuals, or even small groups, who had definite and positive ideologies. However, there prevailed at the time such extreme spiritual isolation, such a total absence of publicity and of the faintest hope for the possibility of change, that the chance of any positive ideology's developing was virtually destroyed at the start.

It can be said that over the course of the last fifteen years at least three ideological viewpoints on which opposition is founded have begun to crystallize. They are "genuine Marxism-Leninism," "Christian ideology" and "liberal ideology."

"Genuine Marxism-Leninism" contends that the regime, having perverted Marxist-Leninist ideology for its own purposes, does not practice real Marxism-Leninism, and that in order to cure the ills of our society it is essential to return to the true principles of that doctrine.

Supporters of "Christian ideology" maintain that the

life of society must return to Christian moral principles, which are interpreted in a somewhat Slavophile spirit, with a claim for a special role for Russia.

Finally, believers in "liberal ideology" ultimately envisage a transition to a Western kind of democratic society, which would, however, retain the principle of public or governmental ownership of the means of production.

Representatives of "Marxist-Leninist ideology" include Alexei Kosterin, who died in 1968, Peter Grigorenko and Ivan Yakhimovich.[17] "Christian ideology" was the inspiration behind the All-Russian Social-Christian Union, whose most notable figure was I. Ogurtsov.° Finally, Pavel Litvinov[18] and, with some reservations, Academician Andrei Sakharov[19] can be considered representatives of "liberal ideology." It is an interesting fact that all these ideologies have, in modified form, also penetrated circles close to the regime.

These ideologies are, however, largely amorphous. No one has yet defined them with sufficient completeness and persuasiveness. Very often they are merely taken for granted by their adherents. The followers of each doctrine assume that they all believe in something held in common, but what that is exactly no one knows. Moreover, these doctrines have no clear limits and often overlap each other. And even in their amorphous forms, they are believed in by only a small group of people. Yet there are many signs that among the broad masses, especially among the working class, the need is felt for an ideology that

---

° I want to make especially clear that by what I have tentatively called "Christian ideology" I mean a political doctrine and not a religious philosophy or an ecclesiastical ideology, representatives of which would be more correctly regarded as members of the Cultural Opposition.

can serve as a base for a negative attitude toward the regime and its official doctrine.*

The Democratic Movement, so far as I am aware, includes representatives of all three of the ideologies that I have described. Its own ideology, therefore, may either be an eclectic fusion of "genuine Marxism-Leninism," Russian Christianity and liberalism, or it may base itself on the common elements in these ideologies (as they are interpreted in the U.S.S.R. today). Evidently the latter is what is happening. Although the Democratic Movement is in its formative period and has no clearly defined program, all its supporters assume at least one common aim: the rule of law, founded on respect for the basic rights of man.

THE NUMBER OF supporters of the movement is almost as indeterminable as its aim. They amount to several dozen active participants and several hundred who sympathize with the movement and give it their support. It would be impossible to give an exact number, not only because it is unknown but also because it is constantly changing. Now, when the regime is "escalating repres-

---

* This is particularly apparent in some of the letters from Soviet citizens received by Pavel Litvinov in reply to the open letter addressed by himself and Larisa Bogoraz-Daniel "To World Public Opinion"[20] during the Galanskov-Ginzburg trial and published in the West by Professor Karel van het Reve.[21]

But perhaps the clearest example is provided by Anatoly Marchenko in his book *My Testimony*. As an ordinary laborer, with seven years' education, he was sent to a prison camp on a trumped-up political charge. There, in search of an ideological grounding, he read through the entire thirty-odd volumes of the works of Lenin. (Apparently this was the only political literature in the camp library.)

sion," the movement will probably go into decline—some of its members will go to prison and others will sever their connections with it. However, as soon as the pressure subsides, the number of members will probably rise rapidly.

More interesting, perhaps, than the number of its supporters is the social composition of the movement. The following analysis is based on a representative sample: those who protested against the trial of Galanskov and Ginzburg.

In essence, the trial served as an occasion for public opinion to voice demands that the regime pay greater respect to the rule of law and to human rights. The majority of those who signed protests against the trial[22] did not even know Galanskov or Ginzburg personally. Thus the vigorous and extensive public protests against the violations of legality at this trial can probably be considered the beginning of the movement.

It can be said therefore to have begun in 1968. But even earlier, at least from 1965, there had been attempts at mass action on behalf of legality. Such were the demonstration of December 5, 1965, in Pushkin Square in Moscow which demanded a public trial for Siniavsky and Daniel (about one hundred persons participated, no arrests were made, but a group of students was expelled from Moscow University); collective letters to various government agencies in 1966 seeking clemency for Siniavsky and Daniel;[23] a collective letter against efforts to rehabilitate Stalin and one protesting the new articles of the Criminal Code (190/1 and 190/3),[24] both of which were signed by prominent representatives of the intelligentsia (their prominence was evidently what forestalled any significant repressive action against the signers); a demonstration on January 22, 1967, in Pushkin Square to demand the liberation of Yuri Galanskov, Alexei Dobrovolsky, Vera Lashkova and Peter Radzievsky, who had been arrested several days earlier (about thirty persons participated, five were arrested and four sentenced to terms of one to three years' imprisonment under the newly approved Article 190/3 of the Criminal Code).[25]

All told, 738 people signed their names to the various collective or individual letters of protest against the Ginzburg-Galanskov trial. The professions of 38 of them are unknown. The following is a compilation of those whose professions are known:

Occupation	Percent
Academics	45
People engaged in the arts	22
Engineers and technical specialists	13
Publishing-house employees, teachers, doctors and lawyers	9
Workers	6
Students	5

In absolute figures, this is the breakdown:

Occupation	Number°
Academics	314

(holders of doctorates, 35; holders of the inter-

° These figures may not be completely reliable and are therefore approximate. I have taken them from *The Trial of the Four*, a collection of documents on the trial of Galanskov, Ginzburg, Dobrovolsky and Lashkova, which was compiled and annotated by Pavel Litvinov.[26] I counted each signer only once, regardless of how many statements and protests he signed. I think that if we counted the persons who signed *all* the statements and letters demanding adherence to the laws, beginning with the letters written during the trial of Siniavsky and Daniel in 1966 and ending with the protests against the arrest of General Peter G. Grigorenko in 1969, the number of signers would be found to surpass one thousand (people, not signatures).

mediate degree of "candidate," 94; without
higher degree, 185)

People in the arts	157

(members of the official unions, 90; nonmembers, 67)

Engineers and technical specialists	92

(engineers, 80; technical specialists, 12)

Publishing-house employees, teachers, doctors and lawyers	65

(editors, 14; other publishing employees, 14;
teachers, 15; doctors, 9; lawyers, 3; retired members of these professions, 7; masters of sport, 1;
priests, 1; chairmen of collective farms, 1)

Workers	40
Students	32

If we accept this social composition of the signers of
letters of protest as typical, it is clear that the basic support of the movement comes from academic circles. Yet,
because of the nature of their work, their position in our
society and their way of thinking, scholars seem to me to
be those least capable of purposeful action. They are
very willing to "reflect" but extremely reluctant to act.
It appears to me that scholarly work requires, in general,
special exertion and total concentration. The privileged
position of scholars in society militates against their taking risks, and the kind of thinking acquired through scholarly work has a more speculative than pragmatic character.
Although at present workers represent a more conservative
and passive group than scholars, I can easily imagine,
some years from now, large-scale strikes in factories, but
I cannot visualize a strike in any scientific research institute.

Further, it is clear that in broader terms the basic support for the movement comes from the intelligentsia. But since this word is too vague, defining not so much the position in society of a person, or a given social group, as the ability of members of this group to perform intellectual work, it would be better if I used the term "middle class."

Actually, we know that in all countries persons of higher-than-average income who practice professions that call for considerable preparation require a certain measure of pragmatic and intellectual freedom for their activities. Furthermore, like any property-owning class, they can only function under the rule of law. They are, consequently, the basic stratum of any society on which a democratic regime bases itself. I believe that the gradual formation of such a class is taking place in our country. It can also be described as the "class of specialists."

In order to exist and carry out its activities, the regime was obliged throughout the postwar period to encourage the country's economy and scientific resources. Since the new scientific and technical personnel are taking on more and more of a mass character in contemporary society, it is they who have bred this sizable class.

Its members have gained for themselves and their families a standard of living that is relatively high by Soviet standards—regular good food, attractive clothes, a nicely furnished cooperative apartment, sometimes even a car and, of course, available entertainment. They pursue professions that assure them a position of respect in society. They achieve a certain level of culture, for instance, opportunities to listen to serious music, to become interested in art or to go regularly to the theater. They possess the ability to assess more or less accurately their own position and the position of society as a whole.

This group includes people in liberal professions, such as writers or actors, those occupied in academic or academic-administrative work, the managerial group in the economic field and so on. They are, as I have said, a "class of specialists." Obviously, this class is beginning to become conscious of its unity and to make its presence felt.

This, too, becomes apparent from an analysis of the authors and signers of the various protests and petitions against the trial of Galanskov and Ginzburg. I do not suggest, of course, that the *entire* "middle class" rose to the defense of the two "renegades" but that *some* representatives of that class have already come to realize clearly the need for the rule of law and have begun, at personal risk, to demand it from the regime.

Thus there exists an influential class, or stratum of society, on which the Democratic Movement could seemingly base itself. But there are at least three interrelated factors that militate strongly against such a development.

Two of these factors spring to mind immediately. First, the planned elimination from society of the most independent-minded and active of its members, which has been going on for decades, has left an imprint of grayness and mediocrity on all strata of society—and this could not fail to be reflected in the "middle class" which is once again taking shape. This elimination, whether through emigration or exile from the country or through imprisonment or physical annihilation, affected all strata of our people.

Second, that section of the "middle class" which most clearly recognizes the need for democratic reforms is also the section that is most imbued with the defensive thought,

"Well, there's nothing I can do anyway" or "You can't break down the wall by beating your head against it." In reaction to the power of the regime, it practices a cult of its own impotence.

The third factor, although less obvious, is most interesting. As is well known, in any country the stratum of society least inclined toward change or any sort of independent action is that composed of state employees. This is natural, because every government worker considers himself too insignificant in comparison with the power apparatus of which he is only a small cog to demand of that apparatus any kind of change. At the same time, he has been relieved of all social responsibility, since his job is simply to carry out orders. Thus he always has the feeling of having performed his duty even though he has done things that he would not have done had he been given a choice.

(On the other hand, the person who issues the orders is equally freed from a sense of responsibility inasmuch as the officials on the level beneath him regard his orders as "good" because they come from above. This creates the illusion among the authorities that everything they do is good.)

For the government worker, the notion of work is narrowed to the notion of a "job." He is an automaton at his post and passive when he leaves it. The government worker's psychology is therefore the one that is most convenient both for the government and for himself.

In our country, since all of us work for the state, we all have the psychology of government workers. Writers who are members of the Union of Writers, scholars employed in government institutions, common laborers or collective farmers are creatures of this psychology just as much as are officials of the KGB or the Interior Ministry.

Therefore, much of the overt and covert protest in the Soviet Union has the character of the dissatisfaction of a junior clerk with the attitude of his superior. This can be seen clearly in the attitude of a number of writers whose names are used in the West as yardsticks of "Soviet liberalism." They are inclined to regard their rights and duties not so much as the rights and duties of a *writer* as those of an "official in the literary department," to use the expression of a character in Dostoevsky.

For example, after Alexander Solzhenitsyn wrote his famous letter about the situation of the Soviet writer,[27] the Moscow correspondent of the *Daily Telegraph* of London, John Miller, asked a well-known Soviet poet in a private conversation whether he intended to join in Solzhenitsyn's protest. The poet said no.

"You must understand," he said, "that this is our internal affair, a question of our relations with the state."

In other words, he regarded the matter not as a question of the writer's conscience and his moral right and duty to write what he thinks, but as a question of internal relations within the Soviet "literary department." He may also protest, but in the manner of a petty clerk, not against the "department" as such but against his rather low salary or against his rude boss. Naturally, this is an "internal matter" and should be of no interest to those who do not belong to the "department."

This curious conversation took place in one of the shops in Moscow where those privileged to have foreign currency are allowed to buy goods not available on the Soviet market.

It goes without saying that the "middle class" is no exception in adopting this government-employee attitude; indeed, this psychology is particularly typical of it by virtue of its position in the middle of the social scale. Many members of this class are simply functionaries of the Communist Party or governmental apparatus. They regard the regime as a lesser evil than the painful process of changing it.

Consequently we are faced with an interesting phenomenon. Although there exists in our country a social class capable of comprehending the principles of personal freedom, rule of law and democratic government, a class that needs those principles and provides the emerging Democratic Movement with its basic contingent of supporters, the vast majority of this class is so mediocre, its ways of thinking are so much those of the government employee, and its intellectually most independent members are so passive that the success of a Democratic Movement based on it seems to me to be gravely in doubt.

It MUST BE SAID, however, that this "paradox of the middle class" is connected in a curious way with a "paradox of the regime." We are aware that the regime underwent very dynamic internal changes in the five years before the war.[28] However, the subsequent regeneration of the bureaucratic elite was carried out by the retention of those who were most obedient and unquestioning. This bureaucratic method of "unnatural selection" of the most obedient members of the old bureaucracy, together with the elimination from the ruling caste of the boldest and most independent-minded, created over the years an increasingly weaker and more indecisive generation of elite. Accustomed to obey unconditionally and without thought in order to attain power, bureaucrats, once they have attained that power, are very good at holding onto it but have no idea how to use it. Not only are they incapable of conceiving new ideas; they regard any novel thought as an assault on their own prerogatives.

Evidently we have reached the sad point where the idea of power is no longer connected with either a doctrine, the personality of a leader or a tradition, but only with power itself. Every governmental institution and position is sustained by no other force than the realization that it is an essential part of the existing system.

Naturally, self-preservation is bound to be the only aim of such a regime, at least in its domestic policy. This has come to mean the self-preservation of the bureaucratic elite. In order to remain in power, the regime must change and evolve, but in order to preserve itself, everything must remain unchanged. The contradiction can be noted particularly in the case of the "economic reform," which is being carried out so slowly and yet is so vital to the regime.[29]

Self-preservation is clearly the dominant drive. The regime wants neither to "restore Stalinism" nor to "persecute the intelligentsia" nor to "render fraternal assistance" to those who have not asked for it, like Czechoslovakia. The only thing it wants is for everything to go on as before: authorities to be recognized, the intelligentsia to keep quiet, no rocking of the system by dangerous and unfamiliar reforms.

The regime is not on the attack but on the defense. Its motto is: "Don't touch us and we won't touch you." Its aim: Let everything be as it was. This is probably the most humane objective the regime has set for itself in the last half-century, but it is also the least appealing.

Thus we have a passive bureaucratic elite opposed to a passive "middle class." Moreover, however passive the elite is, it really does not need to make any changes, and in theory it could remain in power for a very long time, getting away with only the slightest concessions and minor measures of repression.

It is clear that a regime in such a quasi-stable condition requires a definite legal framework, based either on a tacit understanding by all members of society of what is required of them or on written law. In the days of Stalin and even of Khrushchev, there was a sense of direction emanating from above and felt by all, which guided every official unerringly to an awareness of what was currently required of him (reinforced, however, by special instructions) and enabled everyone else to sense what was expected of him. At the same time there existed a "décor" of laws from which the authorities chose whatever they needed at any given moment. But gradually, both "from above" and "from below," a desire became noticeable for more stable "written" norms rather than this "tacit understanding." This desire created a rather uncertain situation.

The necessity of a modicum of the rule of law had made itself felt "at the top" earlier, during the period when the role of the state security organs was being curbed and mass rehabilitations were taking place. In the decade beginning in 1954, gradual, though very slow, progress was achieved in the fields both of formal legislation and of the practical implementation of the laws. This took the form of the signing of a number of international conventions and of an attempt to bring Soviet law into some kind of harmony with international legal norms. Furthermore, personnel changes were carried out among investigative and judicial authorities.

This very slow movement toward the rule of law was further retarded by the following factors: First, the authorities, for various reasons of current policy, issued decrees and regulations which directly contradicted the international conventions they had just signed as well as the approved principles of Soviet law. For example, the decree ordering five years of exile and forced labor for persons with no fixed employment, which was approved in 1961, was not made part of the Criminal Code. Then there was the decree which increased the penalty for illegal currency dealing to include death and which was given *de facto* retroactive force.

Second, the personnel changes were carried out on a very limited scale and with little consistency. They were hampered by a shortage of administrative officials who understood the concept of the rule of law.

Third, the professional egotism of the administrative officials led them to oppose anything that might lessen their influence or abolish their privileged position in society.

Fourth, the very idea of the rule of law had virtually no roots in Soviet society and was in blatant conflict with the officially proclaimed doctrines about the "class" approach to all phenomena.[30]

While the movement toward the rule of law, which had

begun "from the top," thus gradually bogged down in a bureaucratic swamp, suddenly voices demanding the observance of the laws were heard "from below." And, indeed, the "middle class"—the only class in Soviet society to understand and to feel the need for the rule of law— had begun, albeit very timidly, to demand that it be treated not in accordance with the current requirements of the regime but on a "legal basis."

It now became evident that in Soviet law there exists, if I may use the term, a broad "gray belt"—activities that the law does not formally forbid but which are, in fact, forbidden in practice—for instance: contacts between Soviet citizens and foreigners; a concern over non-Marxist philosophies or art inconsistent with the notions of socialist realism; attempts to put out typewritten literary collections; spoken or written criticism not of the system as a whole, which is forbidden under Articles 70 and 190/1 of the Criminal Code, but of particular institutions within the system.

Thus two trends are evident today: the efforts of the regime to "blacken" the gray belt—by means of amendments to the Criminal Code, trials designed to serve as examples to others, and instructions to administrative officials on how to enforce existing regulations—and an effort by the "middle class" to "whiten" the belt, simply by doing things that had earlier been considered impossible and constantly referring to their lawfulness.

All this places the regime in a rather awkward situation, particularly if one bears in mind that the idea of the rule of law will begin to take hold in other strata of society. On the one hand the regime, in the interests of stability, is constantly forced to observe its own laws, while on the other it is constantly forced to violate them so as to counteract the tendency toward democratization.

This has given rise to two interesting phenomena: mass persecution outside the judicial system and selective judicial persecution. Nonjudicial persecution is exemplified primarily by dismissals from work and expulsions from the party. In the course of one month, for instance, over 15 percent of all those who had signed petitions demanding observance of the law in connection with the trial of Galanskov and Ginzburg were dismissed from their jobs, and almost all those who were party members were expelled from the party.

Selective judicial persecution has the aim of frightening those who might be liable for trial on the same charges. Thus it may happen that persons who have committed a more serious crime—from the regime's point of view—may be allowed to go free, while persons who have committed a lesser infraction may be thrown into prison if this requires less expenditure of bureaucratic effort or the circumstances of the moment make it more desirable.

A typical example was the trial of the Moscow engineer, Irina Belgorodskaia, in January, 1969. She was accused of "attempting to circulate" what the court held to be an "anti-Soviet" appeal in defense of the political prisoner Anatoly Marchenko and was sentenced to one year's imprisonment. At the same time, the authors of the appeal, who publicly acknowledged that they had written and circulated it, were not even called as witnesses.

Another contemptible repressive measure is becoming increasingly widespread—forcible commitment to psychiatric hospitals. This is done in the case both of persons who are completely sane and of those with slight mental disorders who do not need hospitalization or compulsory treatment.

As we can now see, the existence of a "Stalinism without violence," while calming the fears of the people which date from the previous era of violence, inevitably produces a new kind of violence: first, "selective persecution" of malcontents, then "lenient" mass persecution. And what next?

Still, looking back over the last fifteen years, we observe that the process of regularizing the legal system has advanced, slowly but rather steadily, and has gone so far that it will be difficult to reverse it by the customary bureaucratic methods. It is a moot point whether this process represents part of the liberalization of the regime which is —or at least was until recently—supposed to be taking place in our country. After all, it is well known that the evolution of our state and society has gone forward not only in the field of law but also in the economy, in culture and in other areas.

In fact, not only does every Soviet citizen feel that he is living in greater security and enjoying more personal freedom than he did fifteen years ago, but the director of an industrial enterprise now has the right to decide for himself matters that previously were not his to decide, while the writer or theater director works within much wider limits than he did before. The same can be said about almost every area of life in our country. This has given rise to yet another ideology in our society, possibly the most widespread one; it can be called the "ideology of reformism."

It is based on the view that a certain "humanization of

socialism" will take place and that the inert and oppressive system will be replaced by a dynamic and liberal one. This will be achieved through gradual changes and piecemeal reforms, as well as by replacing the old bureaucratic elite with a more intelligent and more reasonable group. In other words, this theory is based on the belief that "Reason will prevail" and that "Everything will be all right."

This is why it is so popular in academic circles and, in general, among those who are not badly off even now and who therefore hope that others will also come to accept the view that it is better to be well fed and free than to be hungry and enslaved. I think that all the American hopes about the Soviet Union are derived from this naïve point of view. We know, however, that history, and Russian history in particular, has by no means been a continuous victory for reason and that the whole history of mankind has not followed an unbroken line of progress.

I would like to illustrate this with a small but typical incident involving my friend Anatole Shub, the former Moscow correspondent of the Washington *Post*. At the end of March, 1969, he told me that in his opinion the situation of the regime was so complicated and difficult that in all likelihood there would be a plenary meeting of the Central Committee of the Communist Party in April. At this meeting, even if no decisive changes were made in the party leadership, at least a new, more moderate and more reasonable policy course would be adopted.

Therefore, he intended to behave with maximum caution before the meeting, so as to avoid being the last American correspondent to be expelled from Moscow before the liberal changes occurred. However, no changes were made in April—if the changes in the leadership in Czechoslovakia are excluded—and Anatole Shub was expelled from Moscow in May.

Of course, Anatole Shub is one of the Americans who best understand Soviet reality, and he may possibly have had some reason for believing that there would be a plenum in April. However, he, too, held the exaggerated American belief in "reasonable changes," which are obviously possible only where life is based fundamentally, even if only partially, on reasonable foundations.

In addition to this faith in reason, Americans apparently also believe that the gradual improvement in the standard of living, as well as the spread of Western culture and ways of life, will gradually transform Soviet society— that foreign tourists, jazz records and miniskirts will help to create a "humane socialism." It is possible that we will indeed have a "socialism" with bare knees someday, but not likely one with a human face.[31]

In my view, the growth of material conveniences of everyday life and economic well-being does not in itself prevent or eliminate oppression. As an example, one may cite such a developed country as Nazi Germany. Oppression is always oppression, but in each country it has its own specific traits, and we can correctly understand the causes that brought it about and that can lead to its elimination only in the historical context of that country.

In my opinion, the trouble lies not so much in the fact that the degree of freedom available to us is minimal as compared with that needed for a developed society, and that the process of liberalization, instead of being steadily accelerated, is at times palpably slowed down, perverted or turned back, as in the fact that the very nature of the process gives us grounds to doubt its ultimate success.

It would seem that liberalization presupposes some kind of purposeful plan, put into effect gradually "from above" through reforms and other measures, to adapt our system to contemporary conditions and lead it to a radical regeneration. As we know, there has been, and still is, no such plan, and no radical reforms have been, or are being, carried out. There are only isolated and uncoordinated attempts at emergency repairs by tinkering in various ways with the bureaucratic machine.

The so-called "economic reform," of which I have already spoken, is in essence a half-measure and is in practice being sabotaged by the party machine, because if such a reform were carried to its logical end, it would threaten the power of the machine.

Liberalization could, however, take a "spontaneous" form. It could come as the result of constant concessions on the part of the regime to the demands of a society that had its own plan for liberalization, and of constant efforts by the regime to adapt itself to the storm of changing conditions all over the world. In other words, the system would be self-regulating: difficulties in foreign and domestic policy, economic troubles, etc., would constantly forewarn the ruling elite of changing conditions.

We find, however, that even this is not the case. The regime considers itself the acme of perfection and therefore has no wish to change its ways either of its own free will or, still less, by making concessions to anyone or anything.

The current process of "widening the area of freedom" could be more aptly described as the growing decrepitude of the regime. The regime is simply growing old and can no longer suppress everyone and everything with the same strength and vigor as before; the composition of the elite is changing, as we have mentioned; the contemporary world, in which the regime is already finding it very hard to keep its bearings, is becoming more complex; and the structure of society is changing.

We can visualize all this in the following allegory: A man is standing in a tense posture, his hands raised above his head. Another, in an equally strained pose, holds a Tommy gun to the first man's stomach. Naturally, they cannot stand like this for very long. The second man will get tired and loosen his grip on the gun, and the first will take advantage of this to lower his hands and relax a bit. In just this way, we are now witnessing a growing yearning for a quiet life and for comfort—even a kind of "comfort cult"—on all levels of our society, particularly at the top and in the middle.

If, however, one views the present "liberalization" as the growing decrepitude of the regime rather than its regeneration, then the logical result will be its death, which will be followed by anarchy.

IF, FURTHERMORE, one regards the evolution of the regime as analogous to the growth of entropy,[32] then the Democratic Movement, which I analyzed at the beginning of this study, could be considered an antientropic phenomenon. One may, of course, hope—and this will probably come true—that the emerging movement will succeed, despite persecution, in becoming influential, will work out a sufficiently concrete program, will find the structure necessary to its goals and attract many followers. But at the same time, I think that its base in society—the "middle class," or, more exactly, a part of the "middle class"—is too weak and too beset by internal contradictions to allow the movement to engage in a real face-to-face struggle with the regime or, in the event of the regime's self-destruction or its collapse as a result of mass disorders, to become a force capable of reorganizing society in a new way. But will the Democratic Movement perhaps be able to find a broader base of support among the masses?

It is very hard to answer this question, if only because no one, not even the bureaucratic elite, knows exactly what attitudes prevail among the wider sections of the population. The KGB, of course, supplies the bureaucratic elite with information, gathered by its special methods, about popular feelings in the country. This information obviously differs from the picture drawn daily in the newspapers. However, one can only guess how true to reality the KGB's information is. It is, incidentally, paradoxical that the regime should devote enormous effort to keep everyone from talking and then waste further effort to learn what people are talking about and what they want.

As I see it, popular views can best be described by the words "passive discontent." The discontent is directed not against the regime as such—the majority do not think about it, or they feel that there is no alternative—but rather against particular aspects of the regime, aspects which are, nevertheless, essential to its existence.

The workers, for example, are bitter over having no rights vis-à-vis the factory management. The collective farmers are resentful about their total dependence on the kolkhoz chairman, who, in turn, depends entirely on the district administration. Everybody is angered by the great

inequalities in wealth, the low wages, the austere housing conditions, the lack of essential consumer goods, compulsory registration at their places of residence and work
and so forth.

This discontent is now becoming louder, and some people are beginning to wonder who is actually to blame. The
gradual though slow improvement in the standard of
living, due largely to intensive housing construction, does
not diminish the anger though it does somewhat neutralize
it. It is clear, however, that a sharp slowdown, a halt or
even a reversal in the improvement of the standard of
living would arouse such explosions of anger, mixed with
violence, as were never before thought possible.°

Inasmuch as the regime, because of its ossification, will
find it increasingly more difficult to raise industrial out-
put, it is obvious that the standard of living in many sectors of our society may be threatened. What forms will
the people's discontent take then? Legitimate democratic
resistance or an extreme form of individual or mass acts
of violence?

As I see it, no idea can ever be put into practice if it is
not understood by a majority of the people. Whether because of its historical traditions or for some other reason,
the idea of self-government, of equality before the law and
of personal freedom—and the responsibility that goes with
these—are almost completely incomprehensible to the Russian people. Even in the idea of pragmatic freedom, a
Russian tends to see not so much the possibility of securing

° For this reason, I believe, the regime did not carry out early in 1969
its intention of raising prices sharply on many goods, preferring instead
a kind of creeping inflation. The possible consequences of sharp price
increases were brought home to the regime by the "hunger riot" in
Novocherkassk[33] after Khrushchev raised the prices of meat and dairy
products.

a good life for himself as the danger that some clever fellow will make good at his expense.

To the majority of the people the very word "freedom" is synonymous with "disorder" or the opportunity to indulge with impunity in some kind of antisocial or dangerous activity. As for respecting the rights of an individual as such, the idea simply arouses bewilderment. One can respect strength, authority, even intellect or education, but it is preposterous to the popular mind that the human personality should represent any kind of value.

As a people, we have not benefited from Europe's humanist tradition. In Russian history man has always been a means and never in any sense an end. It is paradoxical that the term "period of the cult of the personality"—by which the Stalin era is euphemistically designated—came to mean for us a period of such humiliation and repression of the human personality as even our people had never previously experienced.

Moreover, official propaganda constantly makes the utmost effort to set the notion of the "communal" against the notion of the "personal," clearly underlining the insignificance of the latter and the grandeur of the former. Hence, any interest in the "personal," an interest that is natural and inevitable, has come to be regarded as unnatural and egotistical.

Does this mean that the masses have no positive ideas whatever, except the idea of "strong government"—a government that is right because it is strong and that therefore must on no account weaken? The Russian people, as can be seen from both their past and present history, have at any rate one idea that appears positive: the idea of *justice*. The government that thinks and acts in everything for us must be not only strong but also just. All must live justly and act justly.

It is worth being burnt at the stake for that idea, but not for the right to "do as you wish." For despite the apparent attractiveness of the idea of justice, if one examines it closely, one realizes that it represents the most destructive aspect of Russian psychology. In practice, "justice" involves the desire that "nobody should live better than I do" (but not a desire for the much-vaunted notion of equalizing wages, since the fact that many people live worse is willingly accepted).

This idea of justice is motivated by hatred of everything that is outstanding, which we make no effort to imitate but, on the contrary, try to bring down to our level, by hatred of any sense of initiative, of any higher or more dynamic way of life than the life we live ourselves. This psychology is, of course, most typical of the peasantry and least typical of the "middle class." However, peasants and those of peasant origin constitute the overwhelming majority in our country.

As I have observed myself, many peasants find someone else's success more painful than their own failure. In general, when the average Russian sees that he is living less well than his neighbor, he will concentrate not on trying to do better for himself but rather on trying to bring his neighbor down to his own level. My reasoning may seem naïve to some people, but I have been able to observe scores of examples in both village and town, and I see in this one of the typical traits of the Russian psyche.

THUS TWO IDEAS that the masses understand and accept —the idea of force and the idea of justice—are equally inimical to democratic ideas, which are based on individualism. To these must be added three more negative and interrelated factors: first, the continued low cultural level of the greater part of our people, especially in respect to everyday culture; second, the dominance of the many myths assiduously propagated by the mass information media; and, third, the extreme social disorientation of the bulk of our people.

The "proletarianization" of the countryside has created an "alien class"—neither peasant nor working class. They have the dual psychology of the owners of tiny homesteads and of farm hands working on gigantic and anonymous farms. How this class views itself, and what it wants, is known, I think, to nobody. Furthermore, the mass exodus of peasants to the city has created a new type of city dweller: a person who has broken with his old environment, way of life and culture and who is finding it very difficult to discover his place in his new environment and feels ill at ease in it. He is both frightened and aggressive. He no longer has any idea to what level of society he belongs.

While the old social structure in both town and village has been completely destroyed, a new one is only just beginning to form. The "ideological foundations" on which it is being built are extremely primitive: the desire for material well-being (relatively modest from a Western viewpoint) and the instinct for self-preservation. Thus the concept "profitable" is confronted with the concept "risky."

It is hard to tell whether, aside from those purely

material criteria, the bulk of our people possess any kind
of moral criteria—such as "honorable" and "dishonorable,"
"good" and "bad," "right" and "wrong," the supposedly
eternal principles which function as inhibiting and guiding
factors when the mechanism of social constraint begins
to fall apart and man is left to his own devices.

I have formed the impression, which may be wrong, that
our people do not have any such moral criteria—or hardly
any. The Christian ethic, with its concepts of right and
wrong, has been shaken loose and driven out of the
popular consciousness. An attempt was made to replace it
with "class" morality, which can be summarized as follows:
Good is what at any given moment is required by authority.
Naturally, such a morality, together with the propagation
and stimulation of class and national animosities, has
totally demoralized society and deprived it of any non-
opportunistic moral criteria.

As an example, I might cite the unusual increase in
casual thievery (as compared with a decrease in professional theft). Here is a typical case: Two young workers
are on their way to visit friends. Walking along the street,
they see an open ground-floor window. They slip in and
grab some trifle or other. Had the window been shut, they
would simply have passed on without more ado. One
constantly sees people enter a house without a greeting,
eat without removing their hats or swear coarsely in the
presence of their small children. All this is normal behavior and not in the least exceptional.

Thus the Christian ethic, which in Russia had a semi-
pagan as well as official character, died out without being
replaced by a Marxist ethic. (There is not space here to
discuss it at length, but it is worth mentioning that Russia

received her Christianity from Byzantium, which was rigid and moribund, and not from the developing and dynamic young Western civilization. This could not but deeply influence subsequent Russian history.) "Marxist doctrine" was revised and reversed to suit current needs too often for it to become a viable ideology. And now as the regime becomes ever more bureaucratic, it becomes ever less ideological.

The need for an ideological underpinning forces the regime to look toward a new ideology, namely, Great Russian[34] nationalism, with its characteristic cult of strength and expansionist ambitions. Something similar took place at the beginning of the century, when the traditional monarchist ideology was replaced by a narrow nationalism. The Czarist regime even introduced into everyday speech the expression "genuinely Russian people" in distinction to the simpler term "Russian," and inspired the creation of the Union of the Russian People.[35]

A regime grounded in such an ideology needs external and internal enemies who are not so much "class" enemies (for instance, "American imperialists" and "anti-Soviet elements") as national enemies (for instance, Chinese and Jews). Such a nationalistic ideology, although it may prove temporarily useful to the regime, is very dangerous for a country in which those of Russian nationality constitute less than half the total population.

The need for a viable nationalist ideology is not only acutely felt by the regime, but nationalist feelings also appear to be taking hold in Soviet society, primarily in official literary and artistic circles (where they have evidently developed as a reaction to the considerable role of Jews in official Soviet art). Beyond these circles, these feelings have a center of sorts in the "Rodina" (Fatherland) Club.[36] This ideology can perhaps be called "neo-Slavophile," although it should not be confused with the "Christian ideology"—partially tinged with Slavophilism—which we discussed earlier. Its central features are an interest in Russianness, a belief in the messianic role of Russia and an extreme scorn and hostility toward everything non-Russian.

Since it was not inspired directly by the regime but arose spontaneously, the regime regards the new nationalism with a certain mistrust (an example of this is the ban on the film *Andrei Rubliov*[37]), yet at the same time with considerable tolerance. It could become a force to be reckoned with at any moment.

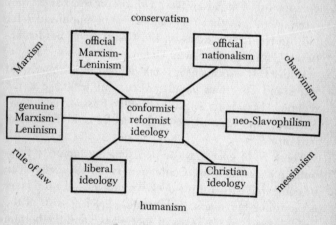

What I have said about the interrelationships of ideologies in contemporary Soviet society may be depicted graphically. The connecting lines in the above diagram show what links these ideologies; it is fairly clear what separates them. "Reformist ideology," if its "ideals" are to be taken in the exact sense of the word, should have been linked most closely with "liberal ideology," but because of its extreme conformism and spirit of accommodation—which can be expressed in the words, "Everything will get better later on; meanwhile we must live"—I have placed it in the center of all the other ideologies.

What, then, are the beliefs and guiding ideas of this people with no religion or morality? They believe in their own national strength, which they demand that other peoples fear, and they are guided by a recognition of the strength of their own regime, of which they themselves are afraid. (It goes without saying that most Russians approved, or regarded with indifference, the Soviet military invasion of Czechoslovakia. On the other hand, they resented deeply that the Chinese went unpunished for the March, 1969, clashes on the Ussuri River border between China and the Soviet Union.)

Under this assessment it is not difficult to imagine what forms and directions popular discontent will take if the regime loses its hold. The horrors of the Russian revolutions of 1905–7 and 1917–20 would then look like idylls in comparison.

There is, of course, a counterbalancing factor to these destructive tendencies. Contemporary Soviet society can be compared with a triple-decker sandwich—the top layer is the ruling bureaucracy; the middle layer consists of the "middle class" or the "class of specialists"; and the bottom layer, the most numerous, consists of the workers, peasants, petty clerks and so on. Whether Soviet society will manage to reorganize itself in a peaceful and painless way and survive the forthcoming cataclysm with a minimum of casualties will depend on how rapidly the middle layer of the sandwich expands at the expense of the other two and on how rapidly the "middle class" and its organization grow, whether faster or slower than the disintegration of the system.

It should be noted, however, that there is another powerful factor which works against the chance of any kind of peaceful reconstruction and which is equally negative for all levels of society: this is the extreme isolation in which the regime has placed both society and itself. This isolation has not only separated the regime from society, and all sectors of society from each other, but also put the country in extreme isolation from the rest of the world. This isolation has created for all—from the bureaucratic elite to the lowest social levels—an almost surrealistic picture of the world and of their place in it. Yet the longer this state of affairs helps to perpetuate the status quo, the more rapid and decisive will be its collapse when confrontation with reality becomes inevitable.

SUMMING UP, it can be said that as the regime becomes progressively weaker and more self-destructive it is bound to clash—and there are already clear indications that this is happening—with two forces which are already undermining it: the constructive movement of the "middle class" (rather weak) and the destructive movement of the "lower classes," which will take the form of extremely damaging, violent and irresponsible action once its members realize their relative immunity from punishment. How long, though, will it be before the regime faces such an upheaval, and how long will it be able to bear the strain?

This question can be considered in two ways, depending on whether the regime itself takes decisive and forthright measures to rejuvenate itself or whether it merely continues to make the minimal necessary changes so as to stay in power, as it is doing now. To me, the second alternative appears more likely because it requires less effort, because it appears to be the less dangerous course and because it corresponds to the sweet illusions of today's "Kremlin visionaries."[38]

However, some mutations within the regime are also theoretically possible: for instance, a militarization of the regime and a transition to an openly nationalistic policy (this could be accomplished by a military *coup d'état* or by the gradual transfer of power into the hands of the military).

Such a policy would no longer disguise the regime's actions beneath the cloak of "protecting the interests of the international Communist movement" in order to make some sort of gesture toward the independent and semi-independent Communist parties in the outside world. (As for the role of the army, it is constantly growing. This can be seen by anyone, for example, who compares today's ratio of military officers to civilians on the reviewing stand on top of Lenin's Mausoleum during parades with what it was ten or fifteen years ago.)

Another possible and very different mutation of the regime could occur through economic reforms and the relative liberalization of the system that would follow such reforms. (This could be achieved by increasing the role in the political leadership of pragmatic economists who understood the need for change.)

Neither of these possibilities appears unlikely on the face of it. However, the party machine, against which either coup would in effect be directed, is so closely intertwined with the military and economic establishments that both groups, if they pursued the aim of change, would very soon bog down in the same old quagmire. Any fundamental change would require such a drastic shake-up in personnel from top to bottom that, understandably, those who personify the regime would never embark on it. To save the regime at the cost of firing themselves would seem to them too exorbitant and unfair a price to pay.

On the question of how long the regime can survive, several interesting historical parallels may be cited. At present, at least some of the conditions that led to the first and second Russian revolutions probably exist again: a caste-ridden and immobile society, a rigid governmental system which openly clashes with the need for economic development, general bureaucratization and the existence of a privileged bureaucratic class, and national animosities within a multinational state in which certain nations enjoy privileged status.

Under these same conditions, the Czarist regime would probably have survived quite a while longer and would possibly have undergone some kind of peaceful modernization had the governing class not fantastically misjudged the general situation and its own strength, and pursued a policy of foreign expansion that overtaxed its powers. In fact, had the government of Nicholas II not gone to war against Japan, there would have been no Revolution of 1905-7, and had it not gone to war against Germany, there would have been no revolution in 1917. (Strictly speaking, it did not start either of these wars itself, but it did its utmost to see that they were started.)

Why regimes that have become internally stagnant tend to develop a militantly ambitious foreign policy I find hard to say. Perhaps they seek a way out of their domestic problems through their foreign policies. Perhaps, on the other hand, the ease with which they can suppress internal opposition creates in their minds an illusion of omnipotence. Or perhaps it is because the need to have an external enemy, deriving from internal policy aims, builds up such momentum that it becomes impossible to halt the growth of hostility. This view is supported by the fact that every totalitarian regime decays without itself noticing it.

Why did Nicholas I need the Crimean War, which brought down the system he had created? Why did Nicholas II need the wars with Japan and Germany? The present regime, curiously enough, embodies traits of the reigns of both Nicholas I and Nicholas II, and, in its internal policy, probably that of Alexander III also. The best comparison, though, is with the Bonapartist regime of Napoleon III. In such a comparison the Middle East corresponds to the latter's Mexico, Czechoslovakia to the Papal States, and China to Imperial Germany.

II

The question of China needs to be considered in detail. Like our country, China has lived through a revolution and a civil war and, like ourselves, has made use of Marxist doctrine to consolidate the country. Also, as in our country, the further the revolution developed, the more Marxist doctrine became a camouflage which more or less concealed nationalist and imperialist aims.

To put it in general terms, our revolution has passed through three stages: (1) international; (2) national, linked with a colossal purge of the old cadres; and (3) military-imperialist, ending with the establishment of control over half of Europe. Then began the "revolution at the top"—the transition from bloodstained Stalinist dynamism, first, to relative stability and then to the present-day stagnation.

It seems to me that the Chinese revolution is passing through the same stages: the international period has been followed by a nationalist period (borrowing from us even its terminology—for instance, the term "cultural revolution," introduced by Stalin). In the logic of events a period of external expansionism must ensue.

My argument may be countered by the assertion that China does not want war and that, despite her very aggressive tone, her actions since the Communist victory in 1949 show her to be a peaceful and not an aggressive power. However, this is not the case.

First, the logic of her internal development has already brought China to the stage of external expansionism. Second, China has already demonstrated her aggressive tendencies toward countries where she did not expect to encounter strong resistance, for example, India. (I am not speaking here about the legality or illegality of China's territorial claims on other countries, particularly India, but only about the methods of their settlement.)

Nevertheless, the impression has been created that China wants to achieve her aims without herself taking part in a global war, but rather by pitting the Soviet Union and the United States against each other, in which case she could then come forward as the arbiter and supreme controller of the fate of the world. This China has failed to achieve, and the fact has long been realized by the Chinese leaders. Evidently this situation will lead, indeed already is leading, to a thorough reassessment of China's foreign policy.

Meanwhile, the relentless logic of revolution is propelling China toward a war which the Chinese leaders hope will solve the country's difficult economic and social problems and secure for China a leading place in the modern world. (Her problems are primarily extreme overpopulation of some areas, hunger and an agriculture that needs extensive rather than intensive development and requires acquisition of new territories.)

Finally, in such a war China will be seeking national revenge for the centuries of humiliation and dependence forced on her by foreign powers. The main obstacle in the way to achieving these global goals is the existence of two superpowers, the Soviet Union and the United States, which, however, do not form a common front against China since they are themselves mutually antagonistic. Naturally, China takes this into account, and launches verbal onslaughts equally against "American imperialism" and "Soviet revisionism and social imperialism." Nonetheless, the real contradictions, and therefore the possibilities for a head-on conflict, are much greater between China and the Soviet Union than between China and the United States.

It may be assumed that the United States will not start a war with China, and China herself will simply be unable to wage such a war in the decades to come. Since she lacks a common border with the United States, she would be unable to exploit her superiority in numbers in a guerrilla war against the United States. Furthermore, she does not have a navy with which she could land troops on American territory. A nuclear-rocket duel—assuming that China succeeds in accumulating a sufficient nuclear arsenal in ten years—would result in mutual annihilation, which would not suit China's purpose at all. Moreover, China is interested in expanding her influence and territory primarily in Asia and not on the North American continent.

Whether the Chinese will manage to attain freedom of action in Asia as long as the United States maintains its might there is another matter. Evidently the United States will on every occasion attempt to stop China from expanding her influence southward in any significant way, and this could lead to exhausting local wars, like that in Vietnam. But it is hardly thinkable that China would be interested in waging wars that will solve nothing, i.e., that would leave the United States itself unharmed.

Getting involved in such wars will seem even more risky to China so long as she has a treacherous foe to the north who would take advantage of any mistake she made. There is still another reason which may restrain China from expanding to the south or east: the overpopulation of these areas and the need either to feed or kill off their many millions of inhabitants.

The north is another matter. There lie the vast, sparsely populated territories of Siberia and the Soviet Far East which were once part of China's sphere of influence. These territories belong to the state that is China's main rival in Asia. It is essential for China somehow to eliminate or neutralize this rival if she is to play a dominant role in Asia and the world at large. Moreover, in comparison with the United States, the Soviet Union is a much more dangerous rival, which, as a totalitarian state with expansionist tendencies, may in one form or another strike the first blow.

China has already had a chance to appraise the methods of her "ally-enemy" during the so-called period of "eternal friendship" between the two countries. Then the Soviet Union, taking advantage of China's economic and military dependence, did all it could to subordinate China completely to its influence. When this failed, the Soviet Union cut off all economic aid and then tried to play on the nationalism of the smaller nations within China's borders.

Evidently Stalin, like Trotsky before him, understood that once the Communists were victorious in China the Soviet Union would in the long run acquire a dangerous enemy rather than an ally. Therefore he worked, on one hand, to spin out the struggle between the Communists and the Kuomintang, which was weakening China, and, on the other, to deepen the divisions within the Communist Party, and in particular to oppose the influence of Mao Tse-tung.

True, there was a time when the Chinese People's Republic and the Soviet Union may have given the impression of being allies, especially since they paid homage to one and the same ideology. However, the absolute antagonism of their national-imperial interests and the conflicting character of the internal processes in each country—"pro-

letarianization" and the rise of a fearsome "revolutionary
curve" in China and "deproletarianization" and a cautious
descent along the same curve in the Soviet Union—quickly
put an end to any pretense of unity.

At first, China wanted to achieve her aims by "peacefully absorbing" the Soviet Union and, after the victory
of the revolution in 1949, offered to unite the two countries
in a single Communist state. With a population three or
four times as great as that of the Soviet Union, China
would of course have secured for herself, gradually if
not at once, a commanding position in such a state and,
more importantly, would have immediately opened up
Siberia, the Soviet Far East and Central Asia to her
colonization.

Stalin did not accept this offer, and the Chinese postponed their plans for several decades; they will now have
to carry them out by military means. Unlike in the above-
mentioned case of the United States, China not only is
capable of waging war against the Soviet Union but will
also enjoy certain advantages in such a war.

Inasmuch as the Soviet Union is at present more powerful militarily than China, the Soviet regime, following a
policy of imposing its will upon China while at the same
time fearing her, will from time to time blackmail her—as
the Czarist regime did Japan at the beginning of the
century—which will merely prompt the Chinese to start
the war first and by the methods that will favor them most.
However, China will not be able to start a war until she
has accumulated considerable stockpiles—although they
may still be smaller than those of the Soviet Union—of
nuclear and conventional weapons.

The date for the outbreak of war will obviously depend

on how soon China can achieve this goal. Taking five years as a minimum and ten as a maximum, we may point to the period between 1975 and 1980 for the beginning of war between the Soviet Union and China. (Those who do not believe that, because of her economic backwardness, China can achieve rapid success in the field of nuclear rocketry should compare the forecasts of American and United Nations experts on how soon the Soviet Union would manufacture atomic and hydrogen bombs with the actual deadlines achieved.)

Having acquired a sizable nuclear arsenal, China will, as I see it, nevertheless start the war by conventional or even guerrilla means, hoping to make use of her colossal superiority in numbers and her experience in guerrilla warfare. She will confront the Soviet Union with the alternative of either accepting the methods of warfare chosen by herself or striking a nuclear blow and receiving one in retaliation.

The Soviet Union will probably choose the former path, because to wage nuclear war, even with an antimissile defense system, would be extremely dangerous, not to say suicidal. At the same time, the Soviet Union's superiority in conventional arms may give the Soviet leaders the impression that the Chinese Army can be destroyed or at least repelled by conventional means.

The actual moment of the outbreak of war may, in fact, be difficult to pinpoint: as her nuclear capability expands, China will increasingly provoke limited skirmishes along her four-thousand-mile boundary with the Soviet Union, infiltrate small detachments into Soviet territory and spark off other sorts of local clashes. These skirmishes will be escalated into total war at the moment most suitable to China. It will thus prove very difficult for the Soviet Union to determine when to launch a nuclear attack against China.

Another logical possibility must also be considered: the Soviet leadership, considering China a potential nuclear rival and aggressor, may decide in favor of a preventive nuclear strike against China's nuclear centers before China has succeeded in amassing enough nuclear weapons to launch a powerful retaliatory blow. The leadership would be able to launch such a strike after fomenting border skirmishes and then presenting China to the Soviet people and world public opinion as the aggressor.

It seems unlikely that a bureaucratic regime would resort to such a desperate measure without also considering the position of the other nuclear powers. But even if this measure is taken, it will not prevent a war; on the contrary, it will signal its beginning. After all, though China's main rocket bases would be destroyed, China would not. She would immediately retaliate by launching an exhausting guerrilla war that would be equally terrible for the Soviet Union whether it was fought on Soviet or Chinese territory.

Strictly speaking, there is still another possibility to consider: an attempt to eliminate China's might by a conventional invasion and occupation of all or part of the country. However, in view of China's great superiority in numbers and her government's complete control over the country, such an invasion seems to me unlikely.

Will the Soviet regime, in the event of a Chinese guerrilla war, decide on the total destruction by nuclear weapons of all China's villages and towns and the whole Chinese population of 800 million people? It is difficult to imagine so apocalyptic a picture, but it is entirely conceivable since, as we know, it is precisely fear which drives people to take the most desperate actions. One can only hope that the other nuclear powers will not allow this to happen, since such an action would endanger the entire rest of the world.

It may be that China foresees the possibility of such a preventive strike. If that is so, she will follow a more cautious policy over the next five years and even flirt with the Soviet Union, something she has not done previously for reasons of internal politics. Diplomatic and possibly party contacts—though meaningless—would follow, ambiguous declarations would be made offering the prospect of reconciliation, and the tone of attacks on "Soviet revisionism and social imperialism" would be slightly softened. At the same time, however, anti-Soviet propaganda within China would not let up, so that the Chinese people would be kept constantly on the alert for critical developments. At the same time, China might seek closer contacts with the United States, and then much would depend on those two countries' relations.

But I believe that a preventive strike will not be made, and for at least two reasons: first, because of the extreme danger of such a strike if it is launched before all other means have been exhausted; and, second, because the possibility of Chinese aggression is not so self-evident as to warrant such risky action. Accordingly, China will accumulate a sufficient nuclear potential to be able to threaten the Soviet Union with reprisals should the latter contemplate using its nuclear advantage for purposes of self-defense. In this way, the Soviet Union will be forced into a guerrilla war of colossal territorial extent along both sides of a four-thousand-mile frontier.

The possibility is not to be excluded that before attacking the Soviet Union China will test her strength against some small neutral country which was once in her sphere of influence and which has a Chinese minority, such as Burma. This would be a trial balloon for the forthcoming "great proletarian revolutionary wars."

Although, presumably, plans have long since been drawn up for the eventuality of a war with China, the Soviet Union, in my opinion, is not prepared, either technically or psychologically, for guerrilla or semiguerrilla warfare. For the last two decades, our country has come to think of war as a clash between two armies equipped with the most modern resources, almost as a "pushbutton war," a war in the West, against countries of Western culture and, finally, against numerically smaller land armies. All this has undoubtedly influenced military thinking in ways that will be very difficult to alter. Furthermore, the minds of the people are better prepared for war against "the Americans" or "the imperialists," for attacks from the air and for a land war in Europe.

It is, of course, very difficult to foretell how the military action will develop, whether Soviet troops will succeed in bursting into China and occupying a considerable part of the country, or whether the Chinese, on the other hand, will slowly but steadily infiltrate into Soviet territory. In any case, the Soviet Union will be facing the same difficulties that its enemies have faced in the past.

In the first place, the actual methods of guerrilla warfare have, from the seventeenth century onward, been the methods applied by the Russians against compact armies invading Russian territory. They have hardly ever been applied against Russian armies invading civilized Europe.

Second, from the very outset the Soviet armies will have to cope with enormously extended lines of communication, because the war will be fought along the Soviet Union's boundaries, thousands of miles from the principal economic and demographic centers.[°]

Third, the Russian soldier, while very often inferior to his adversary in culture, has usually surpassed him in toughness, endurance and an undemanding nature. But these advantages, so important in guerrilla warfare, will now be on the side of the Chinese. The Soviet press is already at work ridiculing the Chinese soldier as fanatical, yet puny and cowardly. Here, however, is the opinion of a Soviet military expert who worked for several years in China:

> The Chinese soldier is superior to ours—hardy, not inclined to grumble and brave. He has immense mobility in the field. For a Chinese soldier to march seventy kilometers in a day is simply a trifle. . . . Our infantrymen, who were quite amazed by the Chinese infantry, came to the conclusion that it is the best infantry in the world.[†]

Finally, since the arena will be the Far East, Siberia and Kazakhstan or adjacent regions on the Chinese side of

---

[°] The seriousness of that problem can be realized by recalling the difficulties the Germans faced during their advance into the Northern Caucasus in 1942, when they were forced to resort to camels to transport fuel for their tanks. At present European Russia is connected with the Far East by only one main railway line, which in many sections consists of only one track. An airlift extended over a long period would prove extremely costly and highly unreliable.

[†] V. M. Primakov, *Notes of a Volunteer*, Moscow, 1967, p. 212.

the border, the war will be waged in areas which are sparsely populated or inhabited by non-Russians. These conditions will offer ample opportunity for guerrilla infiltration as well as serious difficulties in supplying large armies with sophisticated equipment and matériel.

ALL SIGNS THUS point to a war that will be protracted and exhausting, with no quick victory for either side. With this in mind, it is worth considering three problems: the attitude of the United States toward a Soviet-Chinese war; its consequences in Europe; and the resulting situation within the Soviet Union.

Since the Second World War the United States has appeared interested in an agreement and eventual partnership with the Soviet Union. The first step in this direction was made by President Roosevelt and led to the division of Germany and the whole of Europe and to a decade of "cold war." However, this did not discourage the Americans. Both in the Khrushchev era and today they continue to act on the assumption that it will be possible to reach an agreement with the Soviet Union in the not too distant future and together to solve the problems of the world.

This approach is obviously based not on any special sympathies for the Soviet system—although Americans hungrily and impatiently seize upon any insignificant development that can be interpreted as a sign of its "liberalization"—but on the fact that in the present-day world the Soviet Union is the only real force that comes close to matching the power of the United States. It is probably this genuine parity which generates the desire for agreement and cooperation.

From this point of view, however, it is obvious that as China rises in power and influence, the United States will increasingly gravitate toward an agreement with her. American liberals will then begin to find in the regime of Mao Tse-tung or his successors as many attractive features as they saw in the regimes of Stalin or Khrushchev.

By pursuing a policy of encouraging Communism where the people do not want it and opposing it where they do want it, the United States has not only contributed to the division of Europe but also damaged its relations with China. It can be said that its national interests did not oblige the United States to do this. In its relations with China, the United States was guided by the policy of "containing Communism," Communism being seen as an internationally coordinated phenomenon.

In so doing it helped to draw closer together the two Communist giants, the Soviet Union and China. At least ten years had to pass before the great differences between them came to the surface. Furthermore, the United States tied its own hands by supporting the regime of Chiang Kai-shek, which proved to be unviable (it was unable to hold out on the mainland of China and today it could not survive on Taiwan without American support; it is possible, however, that economically, thanks again to the United States, Taiwan is much more developed than mainland China).

If, on the other hand, the United States had supported Mao Tse-tung during the Civil War, this would have averted the rapprochement between China and the Soviet

Union, avoided the Korean War and helped considerably in softening the Communist regime in China.

True, the United States is perhaps beginning gradually to abandon its former policy toward China, and it is difficult therefore to forecast its attitude toward the possible military confrontation between China and the Soviet Union. A great deal will depend also on China's relationship with the United States on the eve of war with the Soviet Union, as well as on the outcome of the Taiwan and Vietnam problems.

Thus, in analyzing the problems of a United States rapprochement with either the Soviet Union or China on a broader historical plane, it should be noted that any such cooperation would have to be based not only on a balance of world forces and the desire on the part of each power to preserve its position in the world, but also on a community of national interests and aims.

I therefore believe that a rapprochement between the United States and the Soviet Union would make sense only after serious steps toward democracy were taken in the U.S.S.R. Until such time, any agreements on the part of the Soviet Union will be motivated either by fear of China or by an attempt to preserve the regime with the aid of American economic assistance (similar to the loans given by France to the Czarist regime, which prolonged its existence by several years), or by the desire to use American friendship to install or maintain Soviet influence in other countries. In addition, of course, there is the interest of both countries in preserving their commanding roles in the world by mutual cooperation. This last objective is apparent, for example, in Soviet-American cooperation to prevent the proliferation of nuclear weapons.

Apart from a few benefits, such a "friendship," based as it would be on hypocrisy and fear, would bring the United States nothing but the same sort of troubles that arose from the cooperation between Roosevelt and Stalin. Cooperation presupposes mutual reliance, but how can one rely on a country that has been capable of no other aim over the centuries than distending itself and sprawling in all directions like sour dough? A genuine rapprochement must be based on similarity of interests, culture and traditions, and on mutual understanding. Nothing like this exists.

What is there in common between a democratic country, with its idealism and pragmatism, and a country without beliefs, without traditions, without culture and without the ability to do an honest job? The popular ideology of our country has always been the cult of its own strength and vastness, and the basic theme of its cultured minority has been the description of its own weakness and alienation. Russian literature is a vivid example of this.

Russia's Slavic state has been created in turn by Scandinavians, Byzantines, Tatars, Germans and Jews. In each case the state has destroyed its creators. It has betrayed all its allies as soon as it found the slightest advantage in doing so. It has never taken seriously any of its agreements. And it has never had anything in common with anyone.

One can hear nowadays in Russia remarks like "The United States will help us because we are white and the Chinese are yellow." It will be very sad if the United States also adopts such a racist attitude. The world's only real hope for a better future lies not in a race war but in interracial cooperation. The best example of this could be good relations between China and the United States.

Undoubtedly, in the course of time China will raise the standard of living of her people considerably and will move into a period of liberalization. This, together with her traditional faith in spiritual values, will make her a remarkable partner for democratic America. In this, naturally, a great deal will depend on the United States itself, on whether it will continue to follow its rigid policy toward China or whether it will correct its previous mistakes and look for new approaches.

If the United States realizes all these possibilities, it will not help the Soviet Union in a war against China, especially since we know that China is incapable of totally destroying the Soviet Union. In such an event, the Soviet Union will face China by itself. And what will our European allies do?

After the Second World War the Soviet Union succeeded in creating along its western frontier a chain of neutral states, including Germany, and thus guaranteed its security in Europe. Such states, with "interim" regimes like the one in Czechoslovakia until 1948, for instance, might have served as buffers between the West and the Soviet Union and guaranteed a stable situation in Europe. Their basic difference from the buffer states of the period between the world wars would have lain in the fact that they could have served not as a *cordon sanitaire* for the West against the Soviet Union, but as a connecting bridge with it.

However, the Soviet Union, by pursuing the Stalinist policy of territorial expansion and the deliberate fostering of international tension, extended its sphere of influence to the farthest possible limit and thereby created a danger for itself. Inasmuch as the existing situation in Europe is maintained only through the constant pressure of the

Soviet Union, it may be assumed that as soon as this pressure lets up or disappears, considerable changes will occur in Central and Eastern Europe. This pressure, we may observe, is sometimes deliberately intensified as in the Berlin crises, and sometimes it takes on a purely hysterical character.

Now as soon as it becomes clear that the military conflict between the Soviet Union and China will be protracted, that all the forces of the Soviet Union are being transferred to the East, and that the U.S.S.R. cannot look after its interests in Europe, Germany will surely be reunited. It is entirely possible that West Germany, in order to hasten this process, will extend support in some form or another to China.

It is hard to predict whether reunification will come about through the absorption of East Germany by West Germany or whether the leaders of East Germany who will follow Walter Ulbricht, understanding what is at stake, will agree to a voluntary merger with Bonn in order to preserve some of their privileges. Whatever the case, a reunited Germany with a fairly pronounced anti-Soviet orientation will create an entirely new situation in Europe.

Clearly, the reunification of Germany will coincide with a process of de-Sovietization in the East European countries and will considerably hasten this process. Paradoxical as it may seem, the Soviet Union can already rely more on President Nixon, the leader of "American imperialism," than on such allies as Ceausescu of Rumania or Dr. Husak of Czechoslovakia. The situation in Eastern Europe today somewhat resembles the situation after the revolutions of 1848, when the democratization that was hoped for did not come about and yet the old regime was shaken.

It is difficult to say how the de-Sovietization of Eastern Europe will proceed and whether it will assume the "Hungarian," the "Rumanian" or the "Czechoslovak" form. However, it will surely result in national-Communist regimes, which in each country will somewhat resemble their pre-Communist regimes—liberal democracy in Czechoslovakia, a military-nationalist regime in Poland and so forth. Meanwhile, several countries at least, such as Hungary and Rumania, will promptly follow their pro-German orientation.

The Soviet Union could evidently prevent all this only by a military occupation of all Eastern Europe aimed at creating a safe rear area for its Far Eastern front. In fact, however, such a rear area would become a second front, that is, a front against the Germans, who would receive the help of the peoples of Eastern Europe—something the Soviet Union could not afford.

It is more likely, therefore, that the de-Sovietized countries of Eastern Europe will dash around like horses without their bridles and, finding the Soviet Union powerless in Europe, will present territorial claims that have long been hushed up but not forgotten: Poland to Lvov and Vilna, Germany to Kaliningrad (Königsberg), Hungary to Transcarpathia, Rumania to Bessarabia. The possibility that Finland will lay claim to Viborg and Pechenga is also not to be excluded. It is probable, as well, that as the Soviet Union becomes more deeply involved in the war, Japan, too, will present territorial claims, first to the Kurile Islands, then to Sakhalin and later, depending on China's success, even to a portion of the Soviet Far East.

Apparently the leaders of the Soviet regime are aware of the threat from Germany and Japan that would arise in the course of a conflict with China, and they might be inclined to take drastic steps toward a rapprochement with those countries. Yet because of the bureaucratic nature of the regime, Moscow cannot be expected to take any decisive steps in this direction.

Briefly, then, the Soviet Union will have to pay up in full for the territorial annexations of Stalin and for the isolation in which the neo-Stalinists have placed the country. However, the events most important to the future of the Soviet Union will occur within the country itself.

NATURALLY, the beginning of a war against China, which will be portrayed as the aggressor, will cause a flare-up of Russian nationalism—"We'll show them!"—simultaneously raising the hopes of the non-Russian nationalities within the Soviet Union. As the war progresses, Russian nationalism will decline while non-Russian nationalism will rise. Indeed, the war will go on for some time without having any direct effect on the emotional perceptions of the people or their way of life, as was the case during the last war with Germany, but all the while exacting a mounting toll of lives.

Eventually the conflict will give rise to a steadily deepening moral weariness with a war waged far away and for no apparent reason. Meanwhile, economic hardships, particularly related to food supplies, will appear, which will be felt all the more deeply because of the recent slow but steady rise in the standard of living.

Since the regime is not lenient enough to permit any

legal channels for the expression of discontent and thus its alleviation, and since at the same time it is not brutal enough to rule out all possibility of protest, there will ensue sporadic eruptions of popular dissatisfaction, or local riots, caused, for instance, by shortages of bread. These will be put down with the help of troops, which, in turn, will accelerate the collapse of the army. Naturally, the so-called internal security troops will be used—and, if possible, troops of a nationality other than that of the population that is rioting, but this will merely sharpen enmities among the nationalities.

As the regime's difficulties mount and as it appears ever more incapable of coping with its tasks, the "middle class" will grow increasingly hostile. The defection of allies and the territorial claims advanced in both West and East will increase the feeling of isolation and hopelessness. Extremist organizations, which will have made an appearance by this time, will begin to play an ever greater role. Simultaneously, the nationalist tendencies of the non-Russian peoples of the Soviet Union will intensify sharply, first in the Baltic area, the Caucasus and the Ukraine, then in Central Asia and along the Volga.

In many cases, party officials among the various nationalities may become the proponents of such tendencies, and their reasoning will be: "Let Russian Ivan solve his own problems." They will aim for national separateness for still another reason: if they can fend off the growing general chaos, they will be able to preserve their own privileged positions.

Meanwhile, the bureaucratic regime, which, with its customary half-measures, will be incapable of simultaneously pursuing the war, solving the economic problems and suppressing or satisfying popular demands, will retreat further and further into itself, losing control over the country and even contact with reality.

A major defeat at the front, or a serious eruption of popular discontent in the capital, such as strikes or an armed clash, will be enough to topple the regime. Naturally, if by this time complete power has passed into the hands of the military, the regime, thus modified, will hang on a little longer. But if it fails to solve the most urgent problems, which in time of war are almost insoluble, it will then fall in an even more terrible manner. If I have determined the time of the outbreak of war with China correctly, the collapse of the regime will occur sometime between 1980 and 1985.

Obviously, the Democratic Movement, which the regime through constant repression has prevented from gathering strength, will be in no condition to take control into its own hands—in any event, not long enough to solve the problems of the country. The unavoidable "deimperialization" will take place in an extremely painful way. Power will pass into the hands of extremist elements and groups, and the country will begin to disintegrate into anarchy, violence and intense national hatred.

The boundaries of the new states which will then begin to emerge on the territory of the former Soviet Union will be extremely hard to determine. The resulting military clashes will be exploited by the neighbors of the Soviet Union—above all, of course, by China.

But it is also possible that the "middle class" will prove strong enough to keep control in its own hands. In that case, the granting of independence to the various Soviet nationalities will come about peacefully and some sort of federation will be created, similar to the British Commonwealth or the European Economic Community. Peace will be concluded with China, which will also have been weakened by the war, and the conflicts with European neighbors will be settled on mutually acceptable terms. It is even possible that the Ukraine, the Baltic Republics and European Russia will enter a Pan-European federation as independent units.

A third possibility also exists—namely, that none of these things may happen.

But what will, in fact, happen? I have no doubt that this great Eastern Slav empire, created by Germans, Byzantines and Mongols, has entered the last decades of its existence. Just as the adoption of Christianity postponed the fall of the Roman Empire but did not prevent its inevitable end, so Marxist doctrine has delayed the break-up of the Russian Empire—the third Rome—but it does not possess the power to prevent it.

Carrying this analogy further, one can also assume that in Central Asia, for instance, there could survive for a long time a state that considered itself the successor of the Soviet Union—a state which combined traditional Communist ideology, phraseology and ritual with the traits of Oriental despotism—a kind of contemporary Byzantine Empire.

But although the Russian Empire has always sought maximum isolation from the world, it would hardly be correct to discuss its fall in a context unrelated to the rest of the world.

Scientific progress is generally considered the fundamental direction of contemporary development, and total nuclear war is regarded as the basic threat to civilization.

And yet even scientific progress, with every passing year consuming progressively more of the world's production, could become regressive and civilization may perish without benefit of a dazzling nuclear explosion.

Although scientific and technical progress changes the world before our very eyes, it is, in fact, based on a very narrow social foundation. The more significant scientific successes become, the sharper will be the contrast between those who achieve and exploit them and the rest of the world. Soviet rockets have reached Venus, while in the village where I live potatoes are still dug by hand. This should not be regarded as a comical comparison; it is a gap which may deepen into an abyss.

The crux of the matter is not the way in which potatoes are dug but the fact that the level of thinking of most people is no higher than this manual level of potato-digging. In fact, although in the economically developed countries science demands more and more physical and human resources, the fundamental principles of modern science are understood by only an insignificant minority. For the time being this minority, in collusion with the ruling elite, enjoys a privileged status. But how long will this continue?

Mao Tse-tung talks about the encircling of the "city" —meaning the economically developed countries—by the "village"—meaning the underdeveloped countries. In fact, the economically developed countries constitute only a small part of the total world population. But what is more, even in the developed countries the "city" is encircled by the "village"—the village in the literal sense of the word or former village dwellers who have only recently moved to the city. And even in the cities the people who direct modern civilization and benefit from it are an insignificant minority.

Finally, in our inner world, too, the "city" is encircled by the "village"—the "village" of the subconscious—and at the first disruption of our customary values we immediately feel it. Is not, in fact, this gap between city and village the greatest potential threat to our civilization?

The threat to the "city" from the "village" is all the greater in view of the fact that in the "city" there exists a noticeable tendency toward the ever greater isolation of the individual, while the "village" is aspiring to organization and unity. This gladdens the heart of Mao Tse-tung, but the inhabitants of the world's cities have reason, as I see it, to worry about their future.

Meanwhile, we are told, Western prognosticators are indeed worried by the growth of the cities and the difficulties brought on by the rapid pace of scientific and technological progress. Evidently, if "futurology" had existed in Imperial Rome, where, as we are told, people were already erecting six-story buildings and children's merry-go-rounds were driven by steam, the fifth-century "futurologists" would have predicted for the following century the construction of twenty-story buildings and the industrial utilization of steam power.

As we now know, however, in the sixth century goats were grazing in the Forum—just as they are doing now, beneath my window, in this village.

April-June, 1969
Moscow and the village of Akulovo

Amalrik's Vision of the End
by Sidney Monas

ON STIFFNECKERY no religious group has held a monopoly. Protestants, Catholics, Jews, Hindus, Moslems and Buddhists have all commanded their fair share, and in Russia both the Orthodox and the Old Believers° were steeped in it, as we who admire the *Autobiography* of that archstiffneck, the Archpriest Avvakum, well remember. Though written in the seventeenth century by a religious leader, the *Autobiography* is a book that bears a striking resemblance to Andrei Alexeievich Amalrik's recent account of his own ordeals, *Involuntary Journey to Siberia.*†

Yet there is a special kind of stiffneckery and a mosaic stiffnecked denunciation of stiffneckery that seem particularly Old Testamental. Amalrik is not Jewish, but his sense of Old Testament traditions runs deep, and, along with Avvakum, he reminds me a little of an uncle of mine.

° Those within the Russian Orthodox Church who resisted the changes Patriarch Nikon attempted to introduce in the middle of the seventeenth century.

† To be published in 1970 by Harcourt, Brace & World, New York.

When I was a boy, this uncle impressed himself indelibly upon my imagination by talking back to policemen and referring them (among other things) to the law and the Constitution, arguing with train conductors (citing the fine print on the back of his ticket), and refusing (as a charity patient) to be treated as a mere "case" by doctors with whom he insistently argued the symptoms and implications of his ailment, which he had studied in medical texts at the public library the day before. He was a small, frail, unpleasant, vehement man, with great reserves of rhetorical denunciation and storehouses of irony and sarcasm. He was uneducated (or rather, confusedly self-educated), sickly and utterly impractical. Although a grudging admiration for his fierce independence might prompt some initial tolerance, almost nobody could stand him for long. He was a failure at everything he tried to do. The most important thing about him, however, was that he refused to acquiesce under any circumstances in the notion of his own insignificance. Poor, sickly and inept, he knew himself to be at a disadvantage in arguing the opposite, and this turned him, in arguing his rights, into an insistent literalist. Although he knew that humanity was higher than the law, he knew, too, that for him the letter of the law was his last refuge in a world that tended to pull everything else from under him. He could practice literalism with great ferocity, just as he could mock it eloquently on other occasions when it was directed at him by others. Andrei Amalrik, the Gentile son of Russia, persecuted in his own country, refuses with the same stiff-necked determination to acquiesce in the notion of his own insignificance.

In the autobiographical account I have mentioned

above, Amalrik reflects at some length on the family name, of Visigothic origin and shared by two Crusader kings of Jerusalem in the twelfth century. He singles out two other putative medieval ancestors. One was a papal legate who, when asked on the capture of a city during the Albigensian Crusade how Catholics could be distinguished from heretics, responded: "Kill them all. God will know his own." The other was Amalric of Bena, teacher at Paris, contemporary of Joachim of Floris, mystic, pantheist, believer in the near approach of the Age of the Holy Ghost— in apocalypse, that is, and the millennium—heretic and martyr. "Possibly our family name originated from one of the followers of this sect of Amalrikans because my great-great-grandfather arrived in Russia in the middle of the last century from the city of Avignon . . . former residence of the popes."

His more immediate ancestors, appropriately enough, included an individualist merchant and others of Old Believer strain. Writing of an uncle who was a friend of the futurist poet Velemir Khlebnikov, Amalrik shows a certain fierce pride:

In 1937, he was arrested. They were prepared to give him five years—at that time the minimum sentence and applied "no matter what"—but it seems that my uncle was an idealist. What for a long time he had considered to be called-for or inevitable in Russia, seemed to him on close examination too disgusting. At the trial he lost control of himself and said it wasn't "a Soviet court, but a fascist torture-chamber!" And he paid for this with his life.

He tells his family's troubles with a weary insistence: his uncle's death, his aunt's, his mother's, his father's grim life, the injustice of it, and finally his father's death while he himself has grimly been serving a term in Siberian exile for "parasitism," the same charge on which the young poet Yosif Brodsky was railroaded in 1964. In painful detail, he tells of himself. His temperament is cautious and plodding in many ways, but he will not give up his right to an independent existence.

Andrei Amalrik is an outsider, and looks at the world with the undeceived, unillusioned squint of the outsider. His view is from the bottom up, the view of persecuted minorities, but it is very steady, brave and unblinking. He is proud of not being a member of the herd, proud of his immunity from the herd instinct. But unlike many of the persecuted, he seems self-confident and secure in his role as outsider. He appears to have come into a tradition of being outside, with an inherited way of looking at things askance, and the acquired capacity to live with persecution and master its secret language. What is more, he has learned to perceive the hollowness and fraudulence beneath the glittering surface of the world of pomp and power. With this come courage, patience and curiosity. He has as well a certain natural piety, a respect for life not to be confused with any kind of churchliness. All together these qualities of mind have endowed Amalrik with a plural consciousness that allows him to participate in events and yet at the same time stand outside them and observe. He tells of his arrest and imprisonment in the following manner:

All that time, from the moment they put me in the car, an intense feeling of curiosity never left me. What would happen next? The other detainees asked me what it was like in prison, and I answered sincerely: Very interesting. Because they knew everything in advance, a powerful melancholy took hold of them. I felt, however, that I had two people alive in me at the same time. One happened to have been plunged into a pretty unpleasant incident, but the other looked on from the sidelines, as if at some actor on the stage, or like the reader of an absorbing book, and he thought: Now let's see what's going to happen next?

There is, in fact, a triple consciousness at work in Amalrik; he has not merely a double viewpoint, for as he participates in an event, he also actively considers it as material for his writing. "And what is an artist," said Flaubert, "if not a triple thinker?"

Amalrik the artist lives intimately with Amalrik the outsider. The questioning view of the world is joined with an unusual sensitivity to the associations and metamorphoses of words. He recounts, for instance, how the prison-slang euphemism for boiled water, "milk," educed in him an unslakable thirst for a glass of fresh milk that was to haunt the days of his captivity. We may, indeed, take this image as symbolic of his entire life predicament. Surrounded by the tired euphemisms of official Soviet language and thought, he yearns for fresh milk, for the dead metaphor resurrected, for the word once again made flesh. Out of this yearning come his revelation, his vision of the end, and of what lies beyond the end.

Not only has Amalrik accepted as his fate the life of an outsider, but even among his own kind—among outsiders—he is something of an outsider. In surveying the work and activity of his friends and allies, he is as merciless, as intolerant of euphemism, as he is when addressing himself to the regime. One of the main reasons for his arrest and enforced stay in Siberia was his advocacy of the painting of Zverev and his acting as intermediary between Zverev and the visiting conductor, Igor Markevich, who arranged a public exhibit of the painter's work in Paris in 1965. Yet in Amalrik's account Zverev emerges as a pathetic and at the same time a somewhat ludicrous figure. Alexander Ginzburg, hero of the Siniavsky-Daniel trial, whose "White Book" made the trial of those two writers known to the world, and who was himself later tried and convicted on dubious charges, is mercilessly criticized for what may have been an early compromise with the political police.

Most recently, Amalrik has written a violent denunciation of the defector, Anatoly Kuznetsov, and although the charges seem to me rigorously just, they could scarcely be considered as fostering a community of opposition; indeed, they have given rise to unpleasant rumors about Amalrik—that he is not really an oppositionist (or why is he still at liberty?) but a police agent. Unfortunately, in the context of Soviet life such rumors often acquire a ring of plausibility. One need only recall that similar rumors circulated, and were believed, about "Abram Tertz"*—along with the rumor that he didn't exist at all, but was the invention of some Polish émigré!

While it is, I believe, a mistake to underestimate the sheer orneriness of Amalrik's character, it is a blind observer who can fail to see its human beauty and heroism in the current Soviet situation. In emphasizing his stubbornness and stiffneckery, I do not mean to deny either his considerable intelligence or his charm, both of which are abundantly, if somewhat intermittently, displayed in his writing. The autobiography, for instance, has a number

---

* The pseudonym of Andrei Siniavsky, under which his writings were published in the West.

of observations as acute and at the same time humorous as the following concerning the police officials who interrogated him about the paintings in his room: "The word 'abstract' or as they pronounced and wrote it, 'obstract,' appealed to them greatly because of its obscurity and ponderousness; and, as an obscure word, it acquired on their lips a kind of sinister meaning." Or his quotation of another police official: " 'What kind of Soviet man are you anyway, not showing any respect for authority?' " Stiffneckery is harder to love than wit; yet it is also essential.

While Amalrik has many gifts, and no doubt these have a broad human dimension, I find it very difficult to imagine him outside the Soviet context in which he lives. Heretic and nonconformist that he is, his heresy and nonconformism nevertheless bear a distinctly Soviet stamp. Nor do I mean to imply by this that there are many, or indeed any, like him in the Soviet Union. Amalrik bears the distinctly local flavor of the talented writer or the prophet.

"Almost ten years ago, I wrote a work on Kievan Rus. Due to circumstances beyond my control, however, I was forced to interrupt my researches on the origin of the Imperial Russian State; now, as a historian, I hope to be compensated for that loss by being a witness to the end of that state." For all the fine irony of this sentence from the opening paragraph of Amalrik's essay, it is an apocalyptic passage and it brings to mind the vision of John of Patmos. It is a Soviet apocalypse.

With the breath of persecution upon him, John of Patmos, an outsider like Amalrik, yet ineluctably a subject of Rome, had conjured up a vision of Christ's judgment of the world that encompassed the collapse and destruction of all that was hollow and corrupt. Amalrik addresses no golden-crowned angel in the clouds. Yet the impulse of his writing is clear: " 'Thrust in thy sickle, and reap: for the time is come for thee to reap; for the harvest of the earth is ripe.' "

At first glance, Amalrik's essay seems to pose rational questions and, in the first part at least, to attempt answers in a supremely detached, analytic manner. True, from the beginning Amalrik hints at the martyrology of his family, his own trouble with the police, his unpublished letter to *Izvestia*; yet the formality of his style and the irony of his tone make the personal element, the element of personal testimony, of something lived through, seem (deceptively enough) somewhat incidental. Indeed, there is an attempt (we discover only later that it, too, is ironic) to set up a kind of social-science framework, as though Amalrik had learned Kremlinology from his foreign-journalist and diplomat friends. Thus we have sociological analysis, with even some show of statistical data, commonsensical political commentary and an appearance of conventional pseudo-scientific orderliness.

What do the changes that began in the U.S.S.R. between 1952 and 1957, but which came to their most dramatic expression in the 1956 "secret speech" of Nikita Khrushchev, really signify? Are they a token of the rejuvenation or decay of the Soviet system? What is the nature of the current situation and what is the likely direction of change in the future? From these questions, others, both explicit and implied, proliferate. What has been the role of Russian literature in the process of de-Stalinization?

Where does the intelligentsia stand? What is its relation to the rest of the population? These are supremely normal questions. Folly lies only in assuming that they can be answered "normally."

Nevertheless, throughout the first part of his essay, Amalrik proceeds as though he were attempting a "normal" answer. There are no red and green dragons here, no "woman clothed with the sun," no whore of Babylon, no "seven trumpets" and no "seven seals." On the contrary, there is every attempt to thrust the traditional symbolism of apocalypse into the background. In the foreground we have rational discourse, detached thoughtfulness; there is civilized irony, the show of objectivity, statistics and even a diagram.

The portrait that Amalrik paints of Soviet society is rather a grim one. At the top is a bureaucratic regime that has lost its original dynamism and stands in danger of stagnation, which in turn poses the threat of a violent and destructive upheaval from below; a regime in which Communist ideology has been suffused with, and stands in danger of being replaced by, Great Russian nationalism, which in turn implies changes—the ascendancy of the military at home and some sort of confrontation politics abroad—that augur ill for the future. In short, he depicts a regime that must introduce fundamental changes in order to save itself, yet is intrinsically incapable of inaugurating such change. At the bottom, he sees a dark unfathomable mass, with enormous destructive potential, which he, unlike other Soviet dissenters—and this is a point I shall return to presently—criticizes ruthlessly, and wherein he sees not much hope. Sandwiched between the paralyzed regime and the dark threatening masses, he sees a middle class where there has indeed been some considerable stir since the days of Stalin, and from which alone, he feels, can emerge any prospect of significant and progressive change in the future.

From the time of Stalin's death, he traces the growth of what he calls a "Cultural Opposition," with its, at first, somewhat abstract, isolated, salon-like character. He dwells at length on the importance of *samizdat*, or the self-publication of authors, the circulation of "underground" manuscripts, in the development of this opposition. He gives an account of the regime's repressive response to *samizdat*, the trials that have resulted and the protests against these trials. From the struggle around *samizdat* he traces a broader and more highly politicized opposition to the regime, which he calls the Democratic Movement. He describes and analyzes the ideological trends within this movement, asks whether these have anything in common and concludes that, yes, they do—a quest for legality, for due process unhampered by political interference, for respect for the individual and the integrity of the individual human personality. Nevertheless, he adds, the movement has not yet found a structure, a coherent set of goals or even in any real sense a membership.

Ultimately, the Democratic Movement depends for its success on what Amalrik calls the middle class, a social formation clearly growing in size and importance and the most likely ground on which the Democratic Movement can find some coherence and structure. Yet for any optimistic view of the future of Soviet democracy, his characterization of this class is devastating. It is, he tells us, a class of specialists, "imbued with the defensive thought, 'Well, there's nothing I can do anyway' or 'You can't break down the wall by beating your head against it.' In reaction to the power of the regime, it practices a cult of its own impotence." Bureaucratic to the core, it is infected with the psychology of the government worker. "Therefore," writes Amalrik, "much of the overt and covert protest in the Soviet Union has the character of the dissatisfaction of a junior clerk with the attitude of his superior." Most tellingly, this middle class has the same resistance to change that characterizes the regime: "Bureaucrats, once they have attained power, are very good at holding onto it but have no idea how to use it."

Americans, with their congenitally optimistic view of history, their confidence in progress, tend to see the emergence of a bourgeoisie as setting the Soviet Union on the road to civil rights, so that every day in every way things will get better and better. How, after its increased exposure to the United States, could the Soviet Union fail to improve? Amalrik, however, strongly doubts that "foreign tourists, jazz records and miniskirts will help to create a 'humane socialism.' It is possible," he adds, "that we will indeed have a 'socialism' with bare knees someday, but not likely one with a human face." In this he could not be more unlike the physicist Andrei Sakharov, who, before the occupation of Czechoslovakia by Soviet troops, foresaw the convergence of the Soviet and American political and social systems, rationality triumphant, ever-increasing democratization on the 1968 Czech model, and a rosy "social-democratic" future for everybody. Amalrik, on the other hand, sees a world coming to an end.

Yet his view of the regime and its relation to the middle class is complex rather than simply pessimistic. On the one hand he projects the image of two men, one holding a gun on the other, who has his hands up. The two are stiff, tense. Inevitably as time passes, the man with the gun relaxes a little; the other lowers his hands and breathes a little more easily. Is the situation better or worse? Yet the real threat of violence at the present time, according to Amalrik, comes not from the man with the gun. The regime is passive; it merely defends itself. "This is probably the most humane objective the regime has set for itself in the last half-century," says Amalrik, "but it is also the least appealing."

Appealing to whom or to what? Here emerges the most striking and original part of Amalrik's essay: his devastating portrayal of the masses. In this there is something of the foreboding, mistrust and "bad conscience" which Raymond Williams° has so acutely singled out in the work of nineteenth-century liberal English novelists like George Eliot, Dickens and Mrs. Gaskell whenever they wrote of the *initiative* of the working classes rather than merely their suffering. Given, however, the power of Russian traditions, the awe and piety in which the *narod* has been held by the intelligentsia and the ongoing devotion of the intelligentsia to the idea of "sacrificing oneself for the people," the significance of Amalrik's departure from populist romanticism is of unusual importance.

He sees in the popular masses an enormous potential for violence, and he finds there a need for an ideology of opposition to the regime which the essentially middle-class Democratic Movement has not succeeded in satisfying. The regime, in spite of its network of secret informers,

° See his *Culture and Society, 1750–1950*, New York, Harper & Row, 1958, pp. 87–110.

knows almost as little of the popular mood as the middle class. "It is paradoxical," writes Amalrik, "that the regime should devote enormous effort to keep everyone from talking and then waste further effort to learn what people are talking about and what they want." Yet it is quite clear that one demand the regime must satisfy if it is to survive is that for a higher standard of living. Success has become problematic, the economy has notably slowed down, and further growth seems difficult to achieve without changes that the regime seems unwilling to make. And failure here, Amalrik insists, "would arouse such explosions of anger, mixed with violence, as were never before thought possible."

Among the popular masses, traditions of freedom, legality, respect for the individual and the human personality have been but weakly developed. "It is paradoxical that the term 'period of the cult of the personality'—by which the Stalin era is euphemistically designated—came to mean for us a period of such humiliation and repression of the human personality as even our people had never previously experienced." Even the myth, believed by much of the intelligentsia, about the peasants' instinct for equality lacks substance, since it turns out in practice to mean little more than a desire to make sure that, as Amalrik puts it, " 'Nobody should live better than I do,' " whereas "the fact that many live worse is willingly accepted." The peasant has shown, traditionally, a "hatred of everything that is outstanding," and of any initiative toward change, and while such attitudes are indeed more typical of the peasantry than of the increasing middle class, the middle class, it must be remembered, draws its new members, in the main, from the peasantry.

Two ideas, according to Amalrik, characterize the Russian peasantry: the ideal of justice (righteousness) and the idea of power. In general, Amalrik's strong sense of sarcasm about presumed peasant virtues would seem to stem from his exposure to peasant life in the Siberian kolkhoz to which he was exiled in 1965. The peasant's "righteousness" —or so this modern Old Believer, this descendant of John and Avvakum by way of Trotsky, tells us—finds someone else's success far more painful than his own failure. It is merely *self*-righteousness, and another aspect of the second idea, the idea of power.

In his account of his Siberian exile, Amalrik has described, with a certain amount of humor and a great deal of painstaking detail, his attempt to become a cowherd. This effort included his having to learn to ride a particularly unmanageable horse. Every day that he set out, Amalrik would talk to the horse, attempting to persuade and cajole him. The peasants laughed at him, Amalrik notes, and they insisted the horse could learn only by being beaten. Like Raskolnikov in Dostoevsky's *Crime and Punishment*, who has a dream in which peasants beat a horse to death, Amalrik seems to be aware that peasant brutality and aggression are based not merely on self-righteousness but also on fear; above all, fear of one's own insignificance. On the national level, this fear objectifies itself in the growing ascendancy of the military and an increasingly militant nationalism; in a rising self-assertiveness in foreign policy and disdain and intolerance for the national minorities within the Soviet Union. And this new militancy coincides with the rising aspirations of previously submerged nationalities; but above all, across

the most immense land frontier in the world, it coincides
and clashes with the rising power of China.

As soon as the subject of China emerges and unfolds,
Amalrik's apocalyptic tone deepens and the imagery of
"the last end" begins to resolve itself in the final metaphor
linking the destruction of Rome with the backwardness of
the Soviet village. One is tempted to object at this point
to Amalrik's omission of certain important issues which in
a purely national, "scientific" analysis should not have
remained unmentioned. Why does Amalrik not deal further
with the Ukraine or specifically with Ukrainian nationalism, surely the most potent separatist force within the
Soviet Union, far more important than similar movements
either in the Baltic or the Caucasus? Why does he not,
after touching on it very lightly, examine the spread of
Christian influence among the Russian masses, especially
by the Baptists and other evangelical sects?

But what does it matter! The vision becomes increasingly personal; more and more the rush of prophecy dis-
places the detachment of analysis. And yet Amalrik's essay
is certainly the more rather than the less compelling for
that. Nor should one discount the rational plausibility of
the argument. China is real, after all, as the newspapers
daily remind us. Nor can it be denied that the Great Russians are a minority in a population of nationalities increasingly vehement in their ethnic passions. The potential
for violence within the Soviet population, the crucial demand for a major improvement in the standard of living
and what seems to be the bankruptcy of the regime in its
current responses to that demand are also, if perhaps just

a little less obviously, facts. Yet the essay is not so much an analysis of the facts as a vision; not a prediction, but a prophecy.

China, whether metaphorically perceived as the "yellow menace" or the "red dragon," is in itself an image of menacing power for the Russian reader. Russian racial feeling about "Orientals"—though often repressed, sometimes successfully, and publicly of course unacknowledged—is strong and widespread. It applies to Chinese, to Japanese, to Uzbeks and other Turkic peoples, and it is sometimes passionately reciprocated. No doubt such feelings go back to the days of the Mongol conquest, the Muscovite princely wars for independence, the imperial expansion of Russia and the subjugation and attempted integration of Asiatic populations. Russia's defeat at the hands of the Japanese in 1904 may have played a certain role here. The writer Andrei Bely, for example, had a pathological fear of "Orientals" and used to hide when he saw a slant-eyed face approach on the street. In his great novel, *St. Petersburg*, set on the eve of the Revolution of 1905, the "Orient"—whether represented by Japanese, or merely Japanese fashions among the upper classes, or the Mongol ancestry of the central characters—stands for the forces of destruction. In all fairness to Amalrik, however, his use of China in an apocalyptic context is absolutely untinged with racism; he does not attempt to invoke this all too easily accessible sense of threat and menace.

The "red dragon" image, mentioned earlier, may be understood in two senses. In the traditional sense it refers to the allegorical beast of the Book of Revelation whose appearance in the Roman world will bring time to a stop. But in a more contemporary sense, it evokes the image of

China which the Russian middle class, with its newly acquired amenities and comforts and pretensions to culture, fears most. Driven by what Amalrik calls "the relentless logic of revolution" (he does not attempt to explain either the basis or the thrust of that logic), China reminds the Soviet middle class of the dangerous and overstrained days of Stalinism from which they hoped they had emerged. They fear on the one hand the threat of Chinese expansionism and on the other the possible influence (which may be exerted negatively as well as positively) of the Chinese on their own regime, i.e., the threat of a backsliding into Stalinist militancy at home. Amalrik, indeed, sees contemporary China in a situation that parallels that of the Soviet Union a generation back, and he concludes from this that Peking has inevitably entered a period of expansionist foreign policy. And yet the China he portrays is far from dragonish. He endows it with the dignity of vitality which he denies to the Soviet Union, and he predicts a rise in its standard of living, followed by a liberalization of its policies and even some kind of genuine partnership with "democratic America"!

While he thus finds in Chinese expansionism the will to live as a saving grace, the Soviet response to it—fundamentally, as Amalrik sees it, the response of militant Great Russian nationalism—betrays, in his view, the *rigor mortis* of an outworn regime. He compares the post-Khrushchevian political leadership with that of Nicholas I and Nicholas II in Russia—bankrupt reigns, followed by extremely drastic social upheavals, in the former case more or less "controlled," in the latter, revolutionary—and of Napoleon III in France.

Mention of the reign of Nicholas I immediately suggests

that odd and lonely figure, whom Amalrik so much resembles—Peter Yakovlevich Chaadaev.

The resemblances are many and striking and go far beyond the fragmentary and "unfulfilled" nature of their work or the fact that both suffered humiliating punishments at the hands of a regime they castigated. Like Chaadaev, Amalrik believes that "salvation is by way of the truth, not by way of the fatherland." Nevertheless, like Chaadaev, he is a patriot; but a patriot with his eyes open. Like Chaadaev, he presents an eloquently devastating portrait of the condition of his native land, and he suffuses it with a moving sense of his own loneliness and isolation. Amalrik even touches on that peculiarly Chaadaevian obsession with the "curse" of Russia's having received Christianity from Byzantium ("rigid and moribund") rather than from the West. As Chaadaev, with restrained dignity and not without a keen critical eye, praises the achievements of Western civilization and contrasts them (perhaps a little too devastatingly) with the "emptiness" of Russia, so Amalrik praises the United States, "a democratic country, with its idealism and pragmatism."

There is, however, an even deeper sense in which they resemble each other. In a brilliant and too little known essay on Chaadaev, Osip Mandelshtam wrote that Chaadaev's praise of the West might well be read rather differently than has normally been the practice. He suggested that wherever Chaadaev writes "West," "Russia" should be substituted. Chaadaev, according to Mandelshtam, was the first Russian educated in the West, imbued with a vision of Western spiritual aims, who returned to Russia with the express intent of implanting there that vision. To Chaadaev Europe's vision meant two things: the goal of unity, a single civilization; and the unity of intellect and spirit. Whether Chaadaev was correct or not in attributing this goal to European civilization is beside the point. He made his own dedication to that purpose clear in the epigraph he used for his famous "First Philosophical Letter"—"Thy Kingdom come!"—invoking thus the establishment of the kingdom of God on earth. When Amalrik praises America, he is projecting, just like Chaadaev, a vision of what Russia could and should be like; which, in turn, should be viewed as merely a stage along mankind's passage toward a brilliant future. Whether or not he is correct in investing such hopes in America, or rather whether America really represents what he sees in it, is of less importance.

If Amalrik's reference to the reign of Nicholas I conjures up the shade of Chaadaev, his reference to Napoleon III suggests Alexander Herzen. The founder of Russian socialism and the man who was as much as any other responsible for shaping the ideology and aims of nineteenth-century revolutionary populism, Herzen was also an important influence on European socialism. In his book called *From the Other Shore*, and dedicated to his son, Herzen attempted to describe his disillusionment with the course of European civilization; his dismay was occasioned by the failure of the revolutions of 1848, which preceded the advent to power of Napoleon III. It has been argued, however, and rather convincingly, that Herzen went to Europe in 1847 *asking* to be disillusioned, and that the events of the following year merely confirmed his desires. Be that as it may, the situation in Eastern Europe today— Amalrik describes it with an explicit reference to 1848 if not to Herzen—bears a striking resemblance to Herzen's description of Europe after the suppression of the 1848 revolutions, "when the democratization that was hoped for did not come about and yet the old regime was shaken."

Herzen wrote much of his book in dialogue form, which helped him to express his divided feelings about the future of European civilization. Europe was, on the one hand, an intimate part of his own identity; on the other, he felt it was doomed and dying and that he must separate himself from it or perish intellectually and spiritually. Only two forces, he thought, could inject new life into this moribund civilization: the European proletariat from within and Russia from without; but it had to be a new and revolutionary Russia, liberated and transformed by the combined efforts of the intellectuals and the instinctively socialist Russian peasants. Russians without and proletariat within: barbarians and Christians. Immediately, the analogy of the fall of the Roman Empire presents itself to Herzen, and his description of the end of Europe —not unlike Amalrik's apocalypse—draws upon the most powerful imagery offered in the book. More important, like Amalrik, he invests his hope in the creative potential of what on the surface seem to be destructive forces—it is better than despair.

With the prophetic-apocalyptic writers of the reign of Nicholas II, Amalrik would at first glance seem to have little in common, however obvious the political analogy might be between his own time and the period preceding the Revolution. Blok, Bely, Merezhkovsky, Rozanov were all to some degree irrationalists and used a kind of language and imagery that was steeped in the fantastic and the surreal. Shestov, who wrote very lucid, straightforward prose, nevertheless bent all his creative energies to an attack on the limitations of reason as a source of knowledge. Amalrik does not seem to resemble these writers. Yet one of his most striking metaphors is an extension of an image provided him by Mao Tse-tung, who "talks about the encircling of the 'city'—meaning the economically developed countries—by the 'village'—meaning the underdeveloped countries." We are all, Amalrik writes, "encircled by the 'village' of the subconscious—and at the first disruption of our customary values we immediately feel it. Is not, in fact, this gap between city and village the greatest potential threat to our civilization?" The style is Amalrik's own, but the metaphor comes from the cultural world of Blok and Bely and suggests a threat on a vast world scale. In an internal sense the metaphor hints at a process analogous to the individual psychological mechanism that Freud has called "the return of the repressed."

In suggesting resemblances between Amalrik's essay and works by other authors, I have so far overlooked one which is rather obvious and which Amalrik himself refers to in his title: George Orwell's *Nineteen Eighty-Four*. Orwell's book was frightening when it first appeared, not merely because the vision of the world it projected was devastatingly dreary, but also because most of its characteristic symptoms seemed already present in the world we knew. Amalrik, like Orwell, discusses not so much the world as it is likely to be in 1984 as his own deepest feelings about the way things are going now. "None of these things may happen," he tells us. Yet if the regime is not moved to change, if the middle class does not find courage, if the Democratic Movement fails to penetrate to the masses, things may turn out even worse.

But prophecy is not prediction. At least the quality of a prophet does not ultimately depend on the accuracy of his predictions—but rather on the power and authenticity of his vision. Nor is apocalypse merely a vision of destruction. John of Patmos saw not only the end of Babylon-Rome, not merely the battle of hosts at Armageddon, the work of the dragons and the abominations of the whore of Babylon. He saw the New Jerusalem as well. His apocalypse was not prediction, but an image of things wished for; a wish that grew out of an experience that was authoritative and compelling and that forces those of us to whom it has been communicated to see in retrospect the congruence of what was wished for and what actually happened.

By the very mode of its telling, *Nineteen Eighty-Four* had to be written from a point of view that lay beyond 1984; the narrator, in other words, writes as though he were chronicling a history of the past and not of the future. In this way, Orwell states that the world where power is pursued exclusively for its own sake, the world of Newspeak and Doublethink, is absurd; and—solid, stable and unassailable as it seemed to those who lived in it—that nevertheless it vanished into thin air and left behind merely a few scraps and ruins for the archaeologist. Amalrik, looking at the un-future of the world he lives in, declares his independence of it, and at the same time his determination to bring about a change. Things may or may not happen, he says, as I have indicated; but unless you cease to acquiesce in the way things are, Armageddon is all you have a right to expect.

Editor's Notes

1. This exile is described in Amalrik's book, *Involuntary Journey to Siberia*, to be published in 1970 by Harcourt, Brace & World in the United States and by Collins-Harvill in England.
2. The term generally used by historians to refer to the territory governed by the Kievan state, formed in the ninth century, as distinguished from the later Russia.
3. This took place in 1952 and appears to have been part of Stalin's preparations for a big new purge.
4. Another indication of a coming purge, this legal frame-up (with strong anti-Semitic elements) took place in early 1953, just before Stalin's death.
5. An opposition Marxist group at Moscow University.
6. Later published in the Russian-language journal *Grani*, No. 58, 1965, Frankfurt, Germany.
7. Published in English as *Journey into the Whirlwind*, New York, Harcourt, Brace & World, 1967.
8. Published in English as *My Testimony*, New York, E. P. Dutton & Co., 1969.
9. Some of these have appeared in English in M. Bourdeaux, *Patriarchs and Prophets: Persecution of the Russian Orthodox*

Church, London, Macmillan. Many others have appeared in Russian-language journals outside the Soviet Union.

10. Poet and translator from the Polish, one of seven who demonstrated in Red Square against the invasion of Czechoslovakia.

11. See Abram Tertz (Siniavsky's pseudonym), *Fantastic Stories*, New York, Pantheon Books, 1963, and *The Makepeace Experiment*, New York, Pantheon Books, 1965.

12. See *This Is Moscow Speaking*, in Patricia Blake and Max Hayward (eds.), *Dissonant Voices in Soviet Literature*, New York, Harper & Row, 1964.

13. Their arrest took place in September, 1965, and their trial in February, 1966.

14. Published in English as *The Chornovil Papers*, New York, McGraw-Hill, 1968.

15. Published in Russian in *Grani*, No. 52, 1962, Frankfurt, Germany.

16. Published in Russian by Possev-Verlag, Frankfurt, Germany. Most of the materials appear in Max Hayward (ed.), *On Trial: The Soviet State Versus "Abram Tertz" and "Nikolai Arzhak,"* New York, Harper & Row, 1967.

17. For materials by and about Kosterin, Grigorenko and Yakhimovich see Abraham Brumberg (ed.), *In Quest of Justice: Protest and Dissent in the Soviet Union Today*, New York, Frederick A. Praeger, 1970. Grigorenko and Yakhimovich were arrested in 1969 and confined to mental institutions.

18. See his book, *The Demonstration on Pushkin Square*, London, Collins-Harvill; also, Brumberg, *op. cit.*

19. See his book, *Progress, Coexistence and Intellectual Freedom*, with an Introduction by Harrison E. Salisbury, New York, E. P. Dutton & Co., 1968.

20. See Brumberg, *op. cit.* Larisa Bogoraz-Daniel, the wife of the imprisoned Yuli Daniel, was exiled to Siberia, along with Litvinov, for participating in the Red Square demonstration against the invasion of Czechoslovakia.

21. K. van het Reve (ed.), *Letters and Telegrams to Pavel M. Litvinov*, Reidel, Holland.

22. See Brumberg, *op. cit.*

23. See Hayward, *op. cit.*

24. See van het Reve, *op. cit.*

25. See Litvinov, *op. cit.*

26. To be published in the United States by the Viking Press.

27. In May, 1967, Alexander Solzhenitsyn addressed an open letter to the Fourth Congress of Soviet Writers demanding the abolition of censorship.

28. A reference to Stalin's purges of the entire Soviet hierarchy.

29. The "economic reform" of 1965, involving some decentralization of decision-making.

30. This approach involves always putting the interests of "the working class"—in reality, of the regime—above all others.

31. A reference to the slogan used by Czechoslovak reformist leaders in setting forth their aims.

32. Entropy: degeneration toward an ultimate state of inert uniformity.

33. This took place in June, 1962. Several hundreds of the rioters were shot down. Novocherkassk is in southern Russia, near Rostov-on-Don.

34. The great Russians constitute the bulk of the Slavic population of the Soviet Union. They are ethnically distinct from the other Slavs on Soviet territory, such as the Ukrainians and Belorussians.

35. A patriotic and chauvinistic Russian society formed at the beginning of this century. It organized pogroms against the Jews, often with official encouragement.

36. A club whose members glorify Russian culture and its history.

37. A film about the medieval Russian icon painter of this name. It has been shown outside the U.S.S.R.

38. A phrase used often in the past to describe admiringly Lenin and the early Bolshevik leaders.

An Open Letter to Kuznetsov

Dear Anatoli Vasilevich,

I wanted to write to you as soon as I heard over the radio your appeal to people in general—and also to me—and your article 'The Russian Writer and the KGB'. I did not do this at once because I was living in the countryside from where my letter would scarcely reach you. But perhaps it has turned out for the best that I am writing to you several months later. First, I have heard of (I have not yet read) your other letters to the Pen Club and to Mr Miller and have been able to understand you better.

Second, it might have appeared that my voice—a voice which comes to you from the country which you have forsaken—would have sounded forth at the same time as the voices of those people in the West who condemned you for your flight and the method you chose for it.

This is not altogether so. I believe that if you as a writer were unable to work here or to publish your books in the form in which you wrote them, then it was not only your right but in a certain sense also your duty as a writer to leave this place. And if you were not able just to pack up and go as anybody in the West can do, then the persistence and cunning which you displayed to this end merits only respect. The fact that you used the methods of your persecutors and twisted them in this way round your little finger is in no way, I think, reprehensible, but the fact that you by your non-return and by means of a frank article turned an ominous report into an inoffensive, amusing piece of work does nothing but harm to the art of reports which exists only in our country.

However, in all that you have written and said while you have been abroad—at any rate as far as I have heard—there are two things that seem to me incorrect and which I therefore want to object to with all frankness.

You speak all the time of freedom, but of external freedom, the freedom around us, and you say nothing of the inner freedom, that is, the freedom according to which the authorities can do much to a man but by which they are powerless to deprive him of his moral values.

But, seemingly, such freedom and the responsibility attributed to it is a necessary prerequisite of external freedom. Perhaps in certain countries the freedom to express his thoughts is as freely available to a man as the air he breathes. But where this does not exist, such freedom, I think, can only come about as the result of a stubborn upholding of his inner freedom.

You say that the KGB has persecuted and blackmailed the Russian writer. Of course, what the KGB has done can only be condemned. But one does not understand what the Russian writer has done to oppose this. To struggle against the KGB is terrible, but what in effect threatened a Russian writer if before his first visit abroad he had refused to collaborate with the KGB? The writer would not have gone abroad—which he probably wanted to do very much—but he would have remained an honest man. In refusing in general to collaborate in this way he would have lost a portion, perhaps a considerable portion, of his external freedom but would have achieved a greater inner freedom. You keep saying they summoned me, they ordered me, the censorship always forced me on my knees, etc. It seems to me that if you had continually made concessions and done what you condemned in your heart you would not have deserved better treatment at the hands of the KGB or the censorship.

I think that I have a right to reproach you for this. I have always tried not to do that which I would condemn in my heart. I not only did not enter the Party as you did, but neither did I join the Komsomol, nor even the Pioneers—although as a small boy I was repeatedly urged to do this. I preferred to be expelled from university and to give up my hope of becoming a historian rather than to correct anything in my work which I myself considered correct. I preferred in general not to send my verses and plays to Soviet publishing houses rather than to mutilate them in the hope that they would be printed.

It would take a long time to relate how the KGB paid attention to me and so I will merely touch on the point you write about. In 1961 I was courteously invited by the KGB to write a general account of the mood of the intelligentsia and I equally courteously refused, upon which the matter ended.

In 1963 I was taken by night to the Lubyanka and ordered to write a report against an American diplomat to the effect that he had subjected me and other Soviet citizens to malicious ideological brainwashing. I again refused, although on this occasion they had threatened me with criminal proceedings. In 1965 I refused outright to talk with them which cost me an exile in Siberia. But the main thing is that by living in this country and by continuing to write and do what I consider right, I can at any moment be sent to prison again or be dealt with in any other fashion. That is why I think I have the personal right to reproach you.

But perhaps I have no right to do this. Above all, because I am almost 10 years younger than you and I was only lightly touched by that most terrible period which coincided with your youth and in which you were formed as an individual. Even now the regime exists, perhaps not only, but mainly, on the interest from the capital of fear amassed in those times. And it is a matter not only of the KGB but the fact that the whole atmosphere of Soviet life and of Soviet education is such that a man is already conditioned to meet with the KGB and to enter into the same relations with it as you did.

Perhaps there is one other reason why I have no right to reproach you, and that is that it can be objected against me that although you repeatedly compromised and even went as far as dishonourable submission, you thereby achieved—albeit in mutilated form—the publication of your books, received recognition as a writer in your own country and thereby made a contribution to its culture, whereas my plays, be they good or bad, belong only to me or to a narrow circle of people; neither in the eyes of the authorities nor in the eyes of society am I a writer and therefore whatever I say or write is of no importance to anybody; that my 'literary honesty' is, in the final analysis, of no more consequence for me than the virginity of a 40-year-old woman.

Again, you may answer my reproach by saying that much in life happens by chance, that it is not only that I have proudly rejected any opportunity of success in the conditions of this regime but that I have been rejected in certain circumstances, that if matters had turned out differently and I had been allowed to publish my article or play after certain changes had been made, would I have stood out against this offer—and having once taken the path of compromise how far would I have gone along it? And would I have written and done things in my life of which I would now be ashamed? This is also true.

Finally, ought one in general to reproach a man who has declared so emphatically that he has broken with his past and has not been afraid to speak of things which many people carry with them to the grave and has thereby shown, albeit partially, how the shameful mechanism of oppression works in our country?

Nevertheless, I do reproach you. Not because I want to criticize you personally, but because I want to criticize the philosophy of impotence and self-justification which runs through all you have said and written in the West. 'I was given no other choice,' you seem to be saying, and this sounds like a justification not only for yourself but for the whole of the Soviet creative intelligentsia—or at least for that 'liberal' part of it to which you belong.

You condemn, directly or indirectly, certain of its representatives, but inasmuch as you do not direct one word of condemnation to yourself, blaming the authorities for everything, I do not understand how you can make any demands on the rest. You want to say that you are all victims of oppression, but it seems to me that no oppression can be effective without those who are prepared to submit to it. I sometimes think that the Soviet 'creative intelligentsia'—that is, people accustomed to thinking one thing, saying another and doing a third—is as a whole an even more unpleasant phenomenon than the regime which gave it birth. Hypocrisy and the acceptance of things as they are foisted on it has become so much a part of it that it considers any attempt to act honourably as either a crafty provocation or madness. I have met people— and you have probably met more—who while secretly hating the authorities do everything they are ordered and, what is more, in doing so they hate the authorities even more. But they have an even stronger hatred for those who, in the words of your letter to Mr Miller, 'struggle noisily against' the authorities.

This is because the enraged authorities, making no distinction, may lash out not only at those who 'struggle noisily' but also at those who 'hate secretly'.

I do not mean that all those who desire greater freedom for themselves and their country should go to Red Square with banners. However, they ought to reject the customary cynicism which equates truth and lies, to believe in some moral values even if they are absurd and to try to acquire inner freedom. How this is to be done must obviously be decided by each person himself. Not everyone can come out openly against those conditions in which we live and maybe this is not always the best method. But it is always better to be silent than to utter falsehoods, better to refuse to publish any of your books than to put out something which is completely contrary to what one had written in the beginning, better to refuse a trip abroad than to become an informer through it or to 'report' by means of a false poem, better to refuse a press conference than to declare publicly that creative freedom exists in our country. If an individual person or the whole country actively wanted to be free they must achieve freedom somehow even if it be by means of non-co-operation with their oppressors. But sometimes to obtain this one must risk even the freedom one has—which, as I understand it, you were afraid to do.

The question which was often put to you in the West, namely, why do the people in the USSR not change the government if it is so bad, seemed to you naïve. This question seems completely reasonable to me. I would reply to it in this way: it is not that the people do not change the government because the government is good but because we ourselves are bad. We are passive, ignorant and fearful; we deceive ourselves with primitive myths and tangle ourselves with bureaucratic ways; we permit our most active citizens to be destroyed; the majority of us do not understand our situation; our intelligentsia is venal, frightened and deprived of moral criteria. Gradually, however, we are beginning to find in ourselves strength—and this means that sooner or later much can change. But you do not talk in this fashion. Willy-nilly, you are trying to create the impression that all struggle is useless and that those who 'struggle noisily' are also hypocrites to a greater or lesser degree when they declare themselves to be 'for the Soviet regime', and as being opposed only to its particular or general short-comings as do Sinyavski or Solzhenitsyn.

Nonetheless, it is Sinyavski who is in prison and it is Solzhenitsyn who is 'persecuted and tormented'. But you, being totally against this regime and therefore a 'true opposition', remained silent and did what you were told by the authorities.

I think that all this is false. The word 'Soviet' by itself is scarcely a good defence against the regime. Perhaps the regime sees the greatest danger in those people who say that they are 'for the Soviet regime' but who understand by 'Soviet regime' not at all what the regime would wish. Not being personally acquainted with either Sinyavski or Solzhenitsyn I cannot judge how far their public position is sincere. It seems to me, however, that it deserves only respect in every case, as does the position of Daniel and many others. As for their books—and I consider Solzhenitsyn the most significant contemporary Russian writer—I suggest that they are not Soviet and not anti-Soviet, but simply literature which wishes to be free.

Judging only by his books, it is impossible to say that Solzhenitsyn is 'persecuted and tormented'—he gives the impression of a man capable of standing out against persecution, he has already once preserved his inner freedom in prison and will evidently do so again if he is once more put in jail. From this we can all derive strength.

And when you say that you wish to write freely and that it was for this that you fled to the West I understand you and I react with respect to the pragmatic coolheadedness with which you managed to do this, but when you try to prove that your 'secret hatred' and open collaboration here constituted 'true opposition', hinting thereby that the opposition of Sinyavski or Solzhenitsyn is false, and at the same time put yourself forward in the West as the herald of this opposition, then I believe that you place yourself in a false position.

The KGB would scarcely be able, as you put it, to destroy the '*samizdat*' in two days and play a cat and mouse game with it. Perhaps the KGB could arrest dozens of '*samizdat*' distributors in a matter of two hours—and the fact that the KGB does not do this proves, it seems to me, not its playfulness (although a game is being played) but the uncertainty in which the KGB and the regime as a whole find themselves. Apart from this, '*samizdat*' is distributed not among individuals as you say but among thousands.

It seems to me that the pitiful role in which the KGB has placed you and many of your colleagues has forced you subconsciously to overestimate its power. You write that we are living in an Orwellian world, but if this is so you have contributed your mite to this world by your submissiveness and mystical attitude towards the KGB.

But, however that may be, you have now entered another world and have brought your 'secret hatred' to a place where it can become open, but, alas, it will provoke neither an answering hatred nor feelings of warm sympathy—rather a sympathetic curiosity, but sometimes, as you have already been convinced, even a hostile curiosity.

It is in connexion with this that I want to address to you my second reproach.

The impression is created that many people in the West have a very poor idea of the actual situation in our country and in particular of the situation of writers. Possibly this is because for people brought up since childhood in a different culture and with different social principles it is as hard to understand another world as it is to speak immediately in another language. Another reason is that information about many facets of our life does not in general reach the West or reaches it in very small quanities. In addition those people whose obligation it is to supply the West with information consciously or unconsciously distort it. Therefore, it is not only the right but also the duty of every Russian who desires that Western public opinion should better understand his country and even by its authority help to achieve greater freedom for it, honestly to inform independent public opinion of what is happening in our country. To inform, but not to seek sympathy and even more not to try to provoke pity as you seem to me to be doing.

I think that your complaints move nobody, just as nobody is moved by my complaints or by those of anybody else, inasmuch as everyone has the strength to bear the misfortunes of others. I believe that the more calmly and objectively we illuminate the situation of the writer in our country and the less dramatically we point out to so-called 'progressive Western public opinion' its dishonestly towards us, the quicker we will be able to destroy the false reputation which the existing regime in our country has been able to create for itself abroad.

I speak of dishonesty because it is dishonest, when one enjoys complete freedom of speech and other freedoms in one's country or is obtaining for oneself greater freedoms and greater influence, to collaborate in any way with a regime which deprives its citizens of these freedoms and of any influence to seek this or that justification for this regime or to enter into any contacts or dialogues with it.

I think that we have no right to condemn these people

because their own problems cause them greater anxiety than all our sufferings, still less have we the right to demand that they crawl into our skins and themselves experience what we have to do. But also we ought not to complain to them, to seek their sympathy or to be offended if we do not find it. We must only speak the truth to them and to anyone who will listen, about the situation in our country. For it is our country itself which needs this in the first instance.

And I think we are still within our rights to say to them: if not only freedom for us but the principle of freedom in general is dear to you, think a little before you travel for the purposes of 'intellectual dialogue' to a country where the very concept of freedom has been distorted and think 10 times before, in admiration of the Potemkin villages, you write reports on Russia which are full of a false significance.

In your desire to convince Western public opinion that the situation of the writers and of the whole people in our country is very grim you repeat several times that we have an allegedly fascist regime. But the point is not whether this is true or not but that until fascism was overthrown and exposed there were many people in the democratic countries who admired fascism or at any rate found in it certain merits. Perhaps they believed that fascism was not suitable for themselves but that it was perfectly all right for the Germans and Italians. Many people also hoped that if it were gradually drawn into the respectable society of various international organizations fascism would give up its bad ways. So that I do not know that your analogies achieve their aim.

I also do not know whether you acted correctly when you asked Mr Miller as President of the Pen Club to occupy himself with the fate of writers in Russia. Mr Miller, irrespective of what sort of writer or person he is, in his position has been compelled to occupy himself not with literature and its fate but with the politics surrounding literature—so it seems looking at the situation from Russia—and in the sphere of these politics has made it his task to bring the Soviet writers' organization into the Pen Club. From the point of view of politics this would possibly constitute a great victory for Mr Miller, but what would it give from the point of view of literature? What gain would there be to our country if Kochetov or Evtushenko were to go to Menton and state that creative freedom exists in the USSR? Is the position of the East German writers better than the position of Soviet writers because East Germany is a member of the Pen Club? In my opinion politics and art are incompatible and even opposed and therefore any politics which are carried out around art not only always harm the interests of art for the sake of purely political motives but also introduce into it a spirit of compromise which is foreign to art.

This is in general what I wanted to say to you. And one more thing: do not take to heart all that you hear in the West. The reproach has been made against you that as a result of your non-return the situation in our country will become even worse, that many of your colleagues will not be able to travel to the West. I do not think that the situation has become worse. The harm lies not in the fact that a routine pseudo-liberal piece of verse will not be published or that its author will not be allowed to travel abroad, but in the fact that many talented poets and prose writers have been deprived of the opportunity of becoming known: some are in general ceasing to write and others are embarking on the path of pitiful conformism. Here, your non-return will change nothing for good or ill. If you can explain this in the West it will be most important.

This is all right, providing you can convince the West that your relations with the KGB were the rule rather than the exception for the Soviet literary milieu. You hint, for example, that several well-known poets were, like yourself, informers. It seems to me, however, that the important thing is not that writers serve the KGB but that literature, like the KGB, fulfils a service function: the important thing is not whether your hints are justified or not but that all this poetic-political deception which flourished in Khrushchev's time and has proved to be not particularly needed by his successors bears as little relation to independent art as the writings of Kochetov. It even appears to me that Kochetov's sincere obscurantism deserves greater respect than the false rebelliousness of those who, together with vodka and caviar, were for a long time an export necessary to the regime.

I am writing to you in answer to articles and letters published openly by you and I therefore consider my letter to be open. Since I wish to have it published I wanted to write as briefly as possible but it has turned out unusually lengthy: either I cannot write or I wanted to touch upon too many things all at once. Nonetheless, I am sending you this letter through the *Daily Telegraph* and I should be very glad if this respected newspaper will publish it. I would wish this above all so that people in the West should know that there is in our country another point of view with regard to your non-return than that which has been expressed in the Soviet press by your former colleagues.

Anatoli Vasilevich, I warmly and sincerely congratulate you on being now in a free country and I hope that this will be a big step for you on your path to inner freedom. Therefore I wish above all for you that your books which are written and published in conditions of freedom will turn out better and more interesting than those which were published under your name in the USSR.

Respectfully,
Andrei Alekseyevich Amalrik,
Vakhtangova Street, no. 5
Apt. 5.
Moscow.

I Want To Be Understood Correctly

Several decades of terror gave rise in my country not only to an atmosphere of fear but an attendant atmosphere of universal distrust and suspiciousness. Consequently when people appeared who dared to do what no one had dared to do earlier, or what was punished by immediate arrest, there were rumours about nearly all of them that if they were acting so boldly it must be by the permission or on the instructions of the secret police. These rumours originated with those who, from congenital or inculcated cowardice, would never themselves dare to do anything displeasing to the regime and could not understand that there might simply be people more courageous or desperate than themselves.

When, therefore, similar rumours about myself reached me I always felt upset but realized that they were inevitable. Also I was well aware that none of my friends or people to whom I am well known would take such a rumour seriously for a second and that none of my ill-wishers would dare to make such a statement publicly knowing they had not a single fact to support it. This is the situation in my own country.

Unfortunately I have discovered that there are also people in the West who follow the logic that 'if someone behaves unlike every one else, then there must be something fishy'. Moreover they permit themselves to give wide publicity to their inventions, while admitting that they have 'no answers, only suspicions'. It seems to me that if one has 'only suspicions' one should not in general publicly blacken someone—these 'suspicions' after all are not merely of academic interest, they concern human honour and dignity.

However since several American newspapers have already published a story that I might be a KGB agent, I would like to make public what I myself think about this.

As I understand this story was first put out by Mr Bradsher

in the *Washington Evening Star* of 26 November 1969. When I first heard about this article I intended to write a short letter to the editor of the newspaper in order to refute the 'suspicions' contained in the article. I assumed that it was written in a manner which, although unpleasant for me, was nevertheless measured and restrained. When I finally succeeded in getting hold of the article and reading it I found that it was nothing but a bucket of slops poured on my head. I do not wish therefore to write to the paper which printed such an article but will give it to American correspondents in Moscow and will be grateful to any American paper which will publish it.

Although Mr Bradsher begins his article in a semi-inquiring tone, it leaves the impression that he is not so much trying to investigate the question of who I am, as deliberately to blacken me. He distorts and juggles with facts, makes unpleasant allusions and reveals a typical police mentality incapable of looking at anything simply and feels himself obliged to seek something hidden and dishonourable underneath. At the same time he is determined not to make any assertion on his own personal responsibility, but refers all the time to certain 'specialists', 'a defector from the USSR', a 'man who knew Amalrik well a few years ago'—all of whom remain anonymous. This sort of article could well appear in *Pravda* with the sole difference that I would be called an agent of the CIA instead of the KGB.

Nevertheless, not being in a position to sue Mr Bradsher for defamation but wishing to defend myself, I will reply to his arguments in detail.

The first argument is my open letter to the 'Soviet novelist Anatoli V. Kuznetsov, who recently deflected to Britain and denounced secret police control of Soviet writers'.

'This letter', continues Mr Bradsher, 'seemed to analysts here intended to destroy Kuznetsov's role in the West as a valiant defender of writers' freedom, and thereby to destroy his usefulness in anti-communist propaganda'. He adds that I 'rebuked him for his own admissions of serving the KGB as an informer'.

In my letter I criticize Kuznetsov by no means for revealing 'secret police control of Soviet writers'. In my eyes Kuznetsov's only courageous act was that he honestly spoke about his co-operation with the KGB and so partially revealed the mechanism for controlling writers. This is what I say in my letter.

Nor do I criticize Kuznetsov for fleeing abroad as some inattentive readers of my letter have supposed. On the contrary I wrote that if he could not work freely in the USSR, it was not only his right but his duty as a writer to escape to a place where he could write what he wanted and publish what he wanted.

I criticize Kuznetsov for the fact that having got abroad he tries to fully justify his activity as an informer and his conformism in the USSR, attributing everything to the cruelty of the regime, and he justifies the cowardly and passive behaviour of the majority of the Soviet intelligentsia which wants to be 'pitied' because it is not free but is not willing to make the slightest effort to seek that freedom. Thus I wrote that if we want to change the regime in our country, we must all take a share of personal responsibility for this.

I hope that Anatoli Vasilevich Kuznetsov has correctly understood the sense of my rebukes which I made not to 'compromise his role in the eyes of the West', but to show him that the independent people of his country neither take the same attitude towards him as the official Soviet press, nor that of those who value him from the point of view of his usefulness to 'anti-communist propaganda'.

It is hard for me to judge whether my letter 'destroys' this 'usefulness' or not, but I should like to say that for me 'propaganda' is the most revolting word, and that when I wrote my letter I was not thinking of communist or anti-communist propaganda but of the dignity of the Russian writer.

Mr Bradsher completely misrepresents my letter. I wrote that judging by his books Solzhenitsyn does not give the impression of a 'persecuted and tormented' man, that he is capable of withstanding any persecution, that he has already retained his inner freedom and dignity in prison once and will, I am sure, retain them again if he is once more put behind bars, and I add that we can all draw strength from Solzhenitsyn's example.

But Mr Bradsher presents this part of my letter thus: 'Amalrik said "it is impossible to say that Solzhenitsyn . . . is persecuted and tormented" and added coolly that he could survive a further term of imprisonment'.

Mr Bradsher distorts my letter to Kuznetsov several more times. He writes: 'Almalrik claimed he preferred to remain silent and suffer than to lie for privileges', and concludes that, since I am silent and at the same time 'apparently do not suffer' nevertheless, this raises a big question. In fact all I said in the letter is that it is better for people who cannot openly protest against the regime simply to keep quiet, rather than write and say the opposite to their own views.

The second argument is my return from Siberia, where I was exiled by the KGB, before my sentence was up. 'In 1966 the Russian Supreme Court revoked the sentence', writes Mr Bradsher, 'and Amalrik returned to Moscow. A revocation was unusual, being allowed to return to Moscow even more usual'. And he goes on: 'Perhaps he bought his way out of Siberian exile by agreeing to co-operate'.

Here again Mr Bradsher distorts the facts or simply does not know them.

The review of sentences is the most ordinary practice, connected not with agreements behind the scenes but with the simple fact that many cases are dealt with extremely incompetently by the lowest organs, and sentences are imposed manifestly without cause, and this forces the higher organs to change them somewhat, even if such cases have been 'cooked up' by the KGB. As for those who were convicted under the decree of 4 May 1961 like me, I do not know of a single case in which a person convicted for political reasons has served his full sentence under this decree, so crudely and unlawfully were these cases dealt with. The poet Joseph Brodski's sentence was reviewed, like mine, and he was able to return to his native Leningrad ahead of time. Much has been written about his case in the West and his poems have been published there. The poet Batshev (from the SMOG group) and the artist Nedbailo also returned to Moscow from exile before their sentences were up. According to Mr Bradsher's logic, one should declare all of them agents of the KGB.

Even more absurd is his assertion that 'permission to return to Moscow is unusual'. Such permission is withheld only in cases where a person is convicted for 'particularly dangerous state crimes' (including those under article 70 of the RSFSR Criminal Code) or is a recidivist. In all other cases, if the convict lived in Moscow before and has relations there who are willing to take him, he can return. Thus in 1962 Ginzburg returned to Moscow after his first term of imprisonment and in 1969 Belogorodskaya returned—I mention those cases which are known in the West. Sometimes even a person convicted under article 70 of the Criminal Code may return. Thus in 1965 General Grigorenko returned to Moscow, released from Leningrad's psychiatric hospital prison. According to Mr Bradsher's logic, all of these are also agents of the KGB.

In the case of a change of review of sentence a return is even more obvious. There is no hope of a review of sentence and practically no hope of a return to Moscow in those cases where the authorities carry out an 'exposé'—with reports in the

press, 'meetings of workers' and so on, as they did with Sinyavski and Daniel and Ginzburg and Galanskov. In the
majority of ordinary cases, such as my own was in 1965,
things are not quite like that. Mr Bradsher is on the whole
badly informed about the law and judicial practice of the
USSR, otherwise he would not have said that I wanted to
'test the law according to which the writers Andrei D. Sinyavski, Yuli Daniel and others were committed to prison for
having sent their works abroad'. There is no law in the USSR
forbidding one to send one's works abroad. Sinyavski and
Daniel were formally convicted not for sending their works
to the West but for their 'anti-Soviet character'. From this
point of view it made no difference whether they published
them in the West or circulated them in typescript among their
friends in the USSR. By my publications I simply want to
prove that, in the Soviet Union as well as in the West, there
is no such law that all prosecutions for this reason are illegal.

'Analysts found it curious', Mr Bradsher further writes,
'that both the 1965 arrest and the May raid (i.e. the search
in 1969—A.A.) occurred in the presence of Americans . . .',
i.e. he wants to give his readers the impression that they were
a special KGB fabrication. In reality I was arrested on 14 May
1965, without any witnesses; even my father, who was gravely
ill, and my friends were only able to find out where I was
after two weeks. If Mr Bradsher were really interested in
the circumstances of my arrest and release—he would first have
to read my book *A Reluctant Journey to Siberia,* to which he
refers in his article and where I wrote in detail about all this. I
think that he would then refrain from his unpleasant and
unproven assertions.

As for the search of 7 May 1969, it really took place in the
presence of American correspondents and that, I think, gave
the KGB no pleasure at all.

The third argument concerns my constant contact with

foreigners and my friendly relations with certain American correspondents in Moscow. 'The dissenters, who have defended Daniel and Sinyavski, who publicly warned of a resurgence of Stalinism and who have denounced the invasion of Czechoslovakia', Mr Bradsher writes, 'are able to do none of these. They are kept by the KGB from such familiarity with Westerners'.

Even according to Mr Bradsher's policeman's logic, one must assume that since these 'public protests and warnings' at any rate became known in the West and received wide publicity, some, if not all, of the 'genuine dissenters' must have had friendly and confidential relations with Westerners in Moscow, in as far as all *samizdat* gets to the West through channels other than Tass and Novosti.

In addition, one cannot draw this conclusion, since it is well known to Western journalists in Moscow that many dissenters have met and meet foreigners and both sides go to each other's houses.

I think that Mr Bradsher has drawn a rather distorted picture of the complete absence of contact between Russians and foreigners, because he himself during the four years of his work in Moscow never once spoke with a single Russian, except for officials, and what is more in general did not know a single word of Russian.

The KGB, indeed, hinders Soviet citizens' contacts with foreigners; in this they are helped by the 'super-wariness' of certain Western correspondents in Moscow, who are afraid to go beyond the four walls of their office and in every encounter with a Russian see 'an agent of the secret police'.

Mr Bradsher because of his gloomy suspicions allows himself other absurdities. He writes, for example, about how my wife and I were able to go on 4 July to a reception at the American Embassy when agents of the secret police were standing at the gates. We went in because we had an invitation, because of which no one would stop us. But we would generally be able to go in answer to any invitation, because, as Mr Bradsher must know well, at the beginning of the reception there are so many guests walking about that none of them is asked for his invitation and the KGB agents are simply not in a position to check on everyone.

Wishing at all costs to discredit me, Mr Bradsher is trying everything to cast me in a bad and distorted light, even using the fact that I like collecting paintings, whilst my wife, an artist, has sold some of her pictures to Americans. 'He has been a purveyor of underground art', thus Mr Bradsher characterizes it. He tried 'to ingratiate himself with the wives of several successive American ambassadors'—he warns later on.

In my opinion only a petty man could write in such a way.

The fourth argument is that my book *1984?* is unpatriotic; I publicize myself through Western journalists, deceived by me, as 'a daring member . . . of the band of dissenters'; Western radio stations broadcast the content of my book to Russian listeners; and all this transfers the indignation at my lack of patriotism on to the 'genuine dissenters'. This cunning plan was drawn up by the department of 'black propaganda' at Novosti, in which I worked, and was then unmasked by the anonymous 'defector from the USSR', who speaks according to Mr Bradsher as an expert on Russian patriotism.

I think that this plan is nevertheless too complicated for mere simple-minded people, who are concerned with Soviet propaganda and counter-propaganda; what is more it would demand the cessation of the jamming of Western broadcasts, just for the narration of my book. But this is not the point.

Here, Mr Bradsher, as in the case of my letter to Kuznetsov, again resorts to direct falsification. I write that the sole hope of the whole world for the best future is not race war, but interracial co-operation, the best example of which would be co-operation betwen the USA and China; Mr Bradsher, in order to prove my 'anti-patriotism', represents this passage as a 'proposal for co-operation between the United States and China which would overthrow the Soviet system'. I wrote that in the event of a prolonged war with China in the border regions of the Soviet Union, tendencies towards national separation would make themselves felt more and more strongly; Mr Bradsher calls this 'an advocacy of regional nationalism in the Soviet Union'. Mr Bradsher also tries in every possible way to play up my work for the Novosti press agency, which is concerned mainly with propaganda in foreign countries. In fact I did work for them, as did thousands of other supernumerary journalists who do not undergo any special test. I interviewed Moscow producers and wrote articles about the theatre and painting; but as soon as the KGB again started taking an interest in me I was immediately dismissed from my work with Novosti, and they even refused to give a reference stating that I had worked for them for two years. After this in order not to be expelled from Moscow again I began distributing newspapers for the Post Office. One has to be endowed with a great imagination or a great lack of information in order to draw from this Mr Bradsher's conclusions.

So far as my 'anti-patriotism' is concerned, without distortion it is possible to find in my book harsh judgments about my country and about my people. It may be that the ordinary Russian, if he were given the opportunity to read or hear my book—and contrary to Mr Bradsher's opinion he will not be given such an opportunity—would find some passages in my book unpatriotic. But I consider that the best patriot is not the man who papers over his country's failings but the man who exposes the wounds so that they can be cured. It may be that it is unpatriotic to criticize one's country and to warn it of threatening dangers, publishing a book abroad for this purpose. But I have no other possibility. And besides, I consider that it is time for my country to overcome its national and social inferiority complex, which leads to every criticism from within or without being considered as something terrible.

I love my country, in which I was born and grew up, and I cannot think without tears of its extraordinary fate. To be separated from it would cause me great grief, but with bitterness I confess that I am not enraptured by my country. If I had been able to make a choice before my birth I should have preferred to be born in a small country fighting for its freedom with weapons in its hands, like Biafra or Israel.

The fifth argument is that in spite of the publication of my books abroad I have still not been arrested. My arrest is a kind of litmus paper which is to indicate whether I am a KGB agent or not. As far as I could understand Mr Bradsher is not the only man who thinks like this.

To pose the question in such terms to me seems extremely immoral. My country is not a Roman arena. I am not a gladiator, and the Western world, in the name of which Mr Bradsher begins to speak with pathos towards the end of his article, is not the Roman plebs, watching excitedly or coolly to see whether the gladiator will really die or whether it is only a circus trick.

When I was writing my books and intending to hand them over for publication I realized that I was risking imprisonment, and I was ready for it and am ready for it now. But I thank God for every day of freedom which is given to me and which I spend at home with my wife. It seems to me that an honourable man who believes in God should not say: 'He has not yet been arrested—that is very suspicious', but rather 'Thank God he has not yet been arrested, that means there is one more free man on earth'.

Mr Bradsher's anonymous 'specialists' have not after all occupied important positions in the secret police of a totalitarian state, and for this reason I think they are scarcely competent to judge who should be arrested straight away and who later. I think that the people in the KGB are reasonably sensible from the police point of view, and that they will arrest me when the fuss abroad has died down, and interest in me and my books has fallen away; and they will not try me for my books but will trump up some minor pretext. And before arresting me they will try blacken my character as they tried to do with all the others. For this reason I think that Mr Bradsher's article will have delighted the KGB.

As far as the date of my arrest is concerned, a bureaucratic regime does not hurry by its very nature and because it knows that no one will escape it. Marchenko was arrested six months after he had begun circulating his books about Soviet prison camps; Grigorenko seven months after his famous speech at Kosterin's funeral; Bogoraz-Daniel and Litvinov seven months after their appeal 'To world opinion'; Yakhimovich 14 months after his letter to Suslov condemning the trials of dissenters; Gorbanyevskaya 15 months after she had taken part in the demonstration in Red Square; and so on. I do not think that they have begun making an exception just for me.

In the West, moreover, the names are well known of Russian writers whose books have been published abroad, and many of whom nevertheless live in freedom; and it is certainly not necessary to commission a special agent to write books in order to 'soften the bad impression created abroad by the savagery of police repressions'.

There are many more inaccuracies in Mr Bradsher's article. He does not even know my name, calling me several times 'Andrei Aleksandrovich' instead of Andrei Alekseyevich. But I think all this is not so important since I believe I have answered all his arguments. All except one, which seemed to me the most offensive.

'Amalrik's name was not found on any of the protests against the trial of Sinyavski and Daniel or the subsequent trials of young dissidents', writes Mr Bradsher, and he draws the conclusion that I 'lack the confidence of other dissidents'.

It seems to me that he ought not write in this way without knowing me and my friends personally. I am bound by ties of friendship, in some cases long-standing, to many of those who fought and are fighting for civil rights and freedom of speech in our country, and the majority of my friends have already paid for their struggle with imprisonment. My friends never doubted me, just as I did not doubt them. I hope that Mr Bradsher wrote this phrase in the heat of the moment, desiring, however he managed it, to give a basis to his suspicions, and that he now regrets it.

But, indeed, I never did sign any collective protests or requests directed mainly towards the Soviet authorities. I never joined any 'dissident group' and never professed to belong to any although I regard these people with great respect, am friendly with many of them, share their aims and try to be useful to them.

When I was finishing my book in a small Ryazan village and watching through the window how after light rain the goats grazed in melancholy fashion, I did not know if the book would ever be published, still less could I foresee that it would attract so much attention. But since this has happened, I wish to be correctly understood.

From childhood the regime under which I was compelled to live was organically alien to me: its culture seemed to be pitiful, its ideology false and the way of life foisted on my fellow-citizens humilating. I am an individualist by nature and my protest has always been a personal one. I always wanted to uphold my human worth and the right to be free myself. But I do not want to be understood as always thinking only of myself. I would like—and perhaps my example helps here— each of my fellow-countrymen also to feel the significance of his own personality. Only then, I think, is a struggle for common interests possible. Because a struggle for 'common interests' by people with a slave psychology can and does lead only to common slavery.

Therefore, I hope that I will be understood in America, a country created by freedom-loving individualists who have come from all corners of the world. I hope that my books, read not between the lines but exactly as I wrote them, will be the best answer to idle talk about them and to outright slander against me.

But if all the same this rumour sticks in the minds of my readers, I will at least be able to find comfort in the old Russian saying 'good repute lies under the pebbles while bad repute dashes along the path'.

An Open Letter to Amalrik

Dear Andrei Alekseyevich,

I have read your essay with great interest and, while leaving detailed conversation about it for the future, would just like to formulate briefly my impressions. The very importance of the matters raised by you restrains me from a hasty or definitive evaluation.

Once again I am delighted by the precision, honesty and detached nature of your position and by the boldness of your act: the very fact of such an initiative is, undoubtedly, a risky step in our conditions, especially at present.

Although I understand and accept the genre of free-ranging reflections which you use, I notice, nevertheless, a difference between the first and second parts of your essay.

The first part makes a very convincing impression by the great detail of its analysis—an analysis of our society which is as yet, in fact, the only one of such breadth and logic. According to my observations, those whom you call 'the middle class' see themselves—and respond to our times—in many ways just as you describe.

However, I cannot fully agree with some of your views, in particular with your forecast of the future of the democratic movement. Although at present its social base is indeed very narrow and the movement itself has been forced to operate in extremely difficult conditions, the ideas proclaimed by it have begun to spread widely throughout the country, and that is the beginning of an irreversible process of self-liberation.

Also, I do not agree with your too one-sided description of the Russian character—but I am not going to charge you with Russophobia, as some critics of your essay are doing in their *samizdat* writings [unofficial underground typescripts]. I see the origin of such charges precisely in your striving for detachment.

I would say that the second part of your essay is less convincing than the first. To predict the future of relations between China and the Soviet Union is certainly a less firmly based undertaking (because of our ignorance of secret diplomacy, the impossibility of reconstructing for ourselves the special atmosphere of international bargaining and agreements, etc.) than to analyse the psychology and ideology of our society, which you have done so successfully.

Lastly, I would like to add to the list of your essay's merits its fine language and the elegance with which you have expounded your thoughts.

Respectfully yours, Pyotr Yakir
Moscow, 28 March 1970.

A Letter to *Der Spiegel*

Dear Editor,
I have read in your journal of 16 March 1970 an article about myself. It was not signed and therefore apparently expressed the view of your journal.

I was surprised that without offering any concrete evidence, you try to suggest to your readers that my book, *Will the USSR Survive until 1984?*, was written in collaboration with the KGB. Such rumours, as far as I know, first appeared in the American paper, the *Washington Evening Star*, in November last year. I wrote a detailed refutation which was published by some American and British papers to which you, while repeating some of the *Star* arguments, do not refer at all.*

I will not try therefore to refute again in detail the slanderous innuendoes repeated by you that my return from exile and the publication of some of my articles by the *Novosti Press Agency* (whose regular employee I never was) had any relation to the KGB. In fact, the only relation to the KGB they had was that in 1965 the KGB exiled me to Siberia and in 1968 it put paid to my journalistic work for the *Novosti Press Agency*, and other Soviet publishing institutions.

All the same, I consider it necessary to reply to some of your allegations, because I think that they are dictated not by ill will, but simply by a complete lack of understanding of the conditions of Russian life.

Thus your comparisons between myself and Gapon and Malinovsky, or your suggestions that the purpose of my critical remarks about the Russian people was to sow discord between the people and the democratic opposition, are not just slanderous but simply nonsensical.

Unlike Gapon and Malinovsky, I am not a member of any organization, I am not trying to provoke anybody to collective action, I am expressing only my own personal views without trying to present them as opinions of the democratic opposition as a whole. As far as my sharp remarks about Russian history and the Russian people are concerned, I made

* Amalrik is obviously unaware here that his refutation, which is published in this issue of SURVEY on pp. 102–110, has not yet appeared in full in the West. Only very brief extracts have been published in the *Daily Telegraph* (23 February 1970) and in the *Guardian* (24 February 1970).

them because I am Russian myself and think that at present my country is more in need of self-criticism than of self-praise.

Nor do I understand why you assert that my book was written for Western readers and that it is not being distributed by *samizdat*. I published the book first in the West and only afterwards I put it into *samizdat* circulation in order to avoid it being published [in a form which might have been distorted] by agencies which are not *bona fide* and which are beyond my control. But since the end of last year my book has had an extraordinary wide distribution through *samizdat*.

Even more nonsensical and slanderous, not just personally to me, but to the whole of independent Russian literature, is the assertion by Mrs. Bronska-Pampuch, approvingly quoted by you, that the sending of *samizdat* publications abroad is controlled, or even carried out by the organs of the KGB. Apart from my writings, in the last few years there were published in the West the novels of Alexander Solzhenitsyn, the memoirs of Anatoli Marchenko, the poems of Natalya Gorbanyevskaya, the essays of academician Sakharov and of General Grigorenko, the documentary compilations on political trials by Pavel Litvinov, and many other texts. Do you seriously think that all these were prepared or sent to the West on the initiative of the KGB?

It is true that the KGB has tried to pass to the West a few manuscripts, but only in such instances when it was against the wishes of the author, or could do him harm, as was the case with *The Banquet of the Victors* by Alexander Solzhenitsyn, or the diary of Svetlana Alliluyeva. But it would be simply dishonest to generalize from such cases.

In my view the KGB does not at all deserve the high marks which you give it in your article. Although the Committee of State Security is undoubtedly a more active and dynamic organization than—say—the Labour and Wages Committee, it is all the same a part of an ossified bureaucratic system and is affected by the general ways of its functioning. (You write that in my critique I do not include the KGB in the 'bureaucratic elite' which it merely supplies with information. Undoubtedly, the supplying of information about attitudes in the country is mainly the task of the KGB *apparatus,* but it does not follow that the top cadres of the KGB do not belong to the elite. Without wishing at all to underestimate the role of the KGB in the Soviet system—a role fully known only to a few people—I would like nevertheless to note that it is now not quite such an exceptional role as the one played by the secret police under Stalin.)

It is quite possible, as you write, that there are nowadays employed in the KGB well-educated and well-informed young men who 'have no illusions'. However, the clumsy provocations in which Victor Louis, whom you also mention, takes part, do not indicate high 'intellectual sophistication' on the part of the KGB. It would be too great an honour for the KGB to have such people as myself among its collaborators.

I think that the rumours that I am a KGB agent are spread by the KGB itself, perhaps partly through its own people in the Russian emigré organizations in the West. The purpose of these rumours is not only to slander me personally and thereby to harm my book which is embarrassing to the bureaucratic regime, but also to advertise the KGB as an organization which knows everything and controls everything.

Such rumours will undoubtedly meet with success among people whose mentality is conditioned by the awe felt vis-à-vis any organization (be it a national, party, or police organization) and by those who, discounting individualism and human personality, believe in the strength of organizations, but not in the strength of man.

The fact that I have not yet been arrested is also used to support these rumours. I can only repeat here what I said before.

After the propaganda failure suffered on the occasion of the Sinyavsky-Daniel trial, the authorities do not want writers' trials which make a lot of noise, focus attention on their books, and create a bad impression throughout the world of the authorities' cruelty. I am not the only Soviet writer who has published abroad and who nevertheless has not been arrested. The authorities are now more interested in the rumours that I am a KGB agent than in my arrest. But I think that as soon as the interest in the West in me and my writings passes, I will be arrested and tried on some false charge or other and that my writings will not even be mentioned at the trial. Of course, they may deal with me in some other way too.

So far, however, I am in fact enjoying greater freedom than many Soviet citizens. But I owe this only to myself. I WANT TO BE FREE. It is precisely because of this that I act as any free man can and should act: I publish my books under my own name and I want to enjoy all the rights of an author. Even in prison, if they do put me in prison, I hope to remain more free than millions of my and your compatriots who in their time, while 'free', shouted 'hurrah' to Stalin and Hitler and believed in the omnipotence of the organizations created by them.

I hope that you will publish my letter in full in your journal.

ANDREI AMALRIK.

2 April 1970
Vakhtangova Street, No. 5
Apt. 5
Moscow.

Andrei Amalrik was arrested in a country house near Moscow on 21st May 1970.

A D D E N D U M :

An Author's Fight for Rights

The following letter, believed to be genuine, was sent in late 1960 to the editors of *The Times* in London, the *New York Times*, *Le Monde* (Paris), *Het Parool* (Netherlands), the *Washington Post*, and the *Los Angeles Times*:

Dear Mr. Editor:

Several publishing houses in Holland, the United States of America, Britain and France either have published or are publishing my books *An Undesired Journey to Siberia* and *Will the U. S. S. R. Survive Until 1984?*, and also my plays. I have made contracts, either directly or through the person whom I have authorized to act on my behalf, with all these publishing houses.

In addition to my desire to publish my books, I have wanted also to prove that a Soviet citizen, like the citizen of any other country, has the right to publish books not issued in his own country, to do this under his own name, to fix personally with the publishers the terms of publication, and to enjoy all author's rights which flow from this.

One of these rights is to receive royalties. Several publishing houses have in fact already sent off to me via the Soviet State Bank, part of the royalties on my books. However, the official Soviet bodies which control the exchange of foreign currency are in fact depriving me of the possibility to receive these royalties.

Referring to a secret instuction, they have stated that I publish my books in the west without the agreement of Soviet official bodies, therefore illegally, and so the rules about the handing over of authors' royalties will not be extended to cover my case. At best they are ready to regard my royalties as a "present", which has been sent to me by someone in the west.

Such an attitude is unacceptable to me, inasmuch as the royalties are not a present but money I have earned. Evidently, however, the attitude is advantageous to the Soviet Government, because a present is subject to a much higher tax than a royalty. In the All-Union Office for the Defense of Authors' Rights, to which I turned for help, they told me that all my publications are absolutely legal, but they refused to help me in defending my rights.

Three years ago I wanted to give to Florence, which had suffered from floods, the royalties on a book of my father's published in the Soviet Union, which I was able to do as his heir. The Soviet Ministry of Finance refused to let me do this, referring to the fact that the Soviet Government is extremely short of foreign currency and cannot therefore convert Soviet roubles into such currency.

Bearing in mind this serious situation of the Soviet Government, I would be able to donate to it a certain sum in foreign currency, but I will never do this under compulsion. Therefore if my author's rights are not going to be respected in the

Soviet Union, I will be forced to ask my publishers not to send royalties through official bodies so unreliable as Soviet ones, but rather to keep them in the west.

I ask your respected newspaper to publish my letter so that I may publicly shame the Soviet Government for the meanness and pettiness which it has shown. While Stalin would have shot me for publishing my books abroad, his pitiful heirs are only up to trying to appropriate a part of my money. This confirms my view about the degradation and growing decrepitude of this regime, which I have expounded in the book *Will the U. S. S. R. Survive until 1984?*.

Respectfully yours,
Andrei Alekseyevich Amalrik.
Soviet Union, Moscow, ul.
Vakhtangova 5, Flat 5.

About the Author

ANDREI ALEXEIEVICH AMALRIK, historian and playwright, was born in Moscow in 1938. In 1963 he was expelled from Moscow University for political reasons. In 1965 he was sentenced for "parasitism" to two and a half years' exile in Siberia. His experiences there form the subject of his book, *Involuntary Journey to Siberia*, soon to be published in the United States. Allowed to return to Moscow at the end of 1966, he has been systematically barred from work by the KGB. Now fatalistically awaiting another arrest, he occupies himself, in his own words, "growing cucumbers and tomatoes." Yet, in reality, living strictly within the law, he has continued to astonish both East and West by openly speaking out against the Soviet system—a moral activist engaged in a personal crusade.

Amalrik has been acclaimed by *Time* magazine as "one of Russia's most promising young writers." *Will the Soviet Union Survive Until 1984?* is, in the words of the London *Sunday Telegraph*, "the most penetrating and balanced analysis of the structure of Soviet society to be produced by anybody, inside Russia or in the West, since the war."

71 72 73   12 11 10 9 8 7 6 5 4 3